Ties That Bind

**Inside the Extraordinary (sometimes knotty)
Food Marketing Continuum**

Dr. Russell J. Zwanka

ISBN-13: 9781688415096

First, start with passion.

Works by Zwanka

Today's Store Walk: Trends, Tips, and Tactics for Today's Food Industry

The ABC's of THC and CBD

The Store Walk: A Walk Through A Grocery Store in Today's Environment

Magic Mushrooms: Future Trend or One-Time Trip?

A Post Pandemic Store Walk

Pandemic Positivity: Turning a Pandemic into a Roadmap for a Positive Life

Food Forethought: 48 Healthy Food Tips for Navigating the Grocery Store

Simple Solutions to Make Customers Feel Like Your Supermarket is Their Supermarket

Ties That Bind: Inside the Extraordinary (sometimes knotty) Food Marketing Continuum

CBD Reality

A note from your professor

CBD Dreams

Public Speaking for Everyone

So, how do I do this Marketing thing?

Marketing in Today's Cuba

A Store Walk

Dr. Z's Guide to Grocery and Cooking and Cool Stuff Like That

Successfully Succinct Stage Speaking

A Marketing Manual for the Millennium

Category Management Principles

Customer Connectivity in Global Brands and Retailers

Requisite Reading for the Renaissance Retailer

Operating in the New Cuba

Food Retail Management Strategic Cases

Would You Shop Here if You Didn't Work Here?

Customers First. Profits Second.

About Dr. Zwanka

Dr. Russell J. Zwanka serves as Director of the Food Marketing Program, and Professor of Category Management and Food Marketing, at Western Michigan University, one of the top Food Marketing programs in the world. Delivering high quality curriculum and applied food marketing skills, along with the Food Industry Research and Education Center, Western Michigan University endeavors to work with the food industry to provide real time solutions; while also helping educate the future leaders of the food industry. Zwanka has previously taught Marketing Research, Personal Selling, Marketing Strategy, Food Marketing, Business Strategy, Global Business, and Marketing Principles.

Having spent a career in the food industry before teaching, Dr. Z conceptualized and formed the Food Marketing Concentration at Siena College; as well as the Food Marketing Track at the State University of New York at New Paltz. Serving as the Chair of the Food Industry University Coalition (FIUC), Zwanka works with other universities teaching Food Marketing, to help educate the future of the food industry. The FIUC is made in part by the generosity of the National Grocers Association (NGA).

Dr. Z is CEO of Triple Eight Marketing, a retail consultancy- helping food organizations re-align around customer lifestyle and orientation. Dr. Z has led the merchandising, marketing, advertising, procurement, and all customer engagement areas for multiple food retail companies domestically and internationally.

Zwanka holds a Doctorate in International Business from ISM in Paris, France. He also holds a Master of Science in Management from Southern Wesleyan University, and a Bachelor of Science in Psychology from the University of South Carolina. Never stop learning….

Dr. Z can be followed at "Dr.Z@TEM888" and www.tripleeightmarketing.com.

Table of Contents

Foreword

It all started when I was fourteen. I can remember the day like it was yesterday. I received a call on the phone that was connected to the wall, and picked up the receiver that was connected by a cord to the phone connected to the wall- giving you a little insight into the timing and my age. And, surprise to anyone under twenty years of age, we did <u>not</u> know who was calling. That little bit of technology would come later. It was my brother, Warren, on the other line. He was calling from Fogle's Food City in West Columbia, South Carolina. Warren worked in the produce department, and wanted to know if I could come down and work a few shifts while the older teenagers went to the beach. Warren had gotten his job because our oldest brother, Merrill, had referred him. In fact, pretty much everyone working at Fogle's Food City had gotten the job because someone in their family had previously worked there. It's what you did in the small independent operators, much like still happens today in IGA stores all over the world. The job? Bag groceries, take them to the customers' cars, and pocket the tips. I would work for tips plus $2.25 per hour, paid with cash from the register. I was underage, after all.

So, that started what was going to be a pretty neat career in the food industry. But, I didn't know it at the time. In fact, once I became of "legal age" and took my rightful place replacing Warren as the "assistant produce clerk" in a department of two of us, the industry was already changing rapidly. Looking back now, the industry has always been changing rapidly. My Produce Manager at the time, Forrest, taught me one of my first lessons in food. When I asked him how to pick out the best watermelon, he told me simply- "tap three and pick the middle one". That little tidbit of wisdom had deeper meaning, and was more prescient, than Forrest probably even knew.

First, **customers are constantly searching for knowledge and insight into what they should eat**. Second, **they seem to trust anyone who acts like they know what they are doing**. The responsibility to take food nutritional guidelines, safety procedures, contamination control, etc. seriously weighs on the merchant or the food purveyor. There is an inherent trust in those who hand us our food. Whatever life lessons I learned, they didn't matter, I was going to the University of South Carolina and majoring in Engineering. I would keep the job until I graduated and would then get a "real job". After a semester in Engineering, I realized quickly that I needed to find another major. Choosing Psychology as my major, I still had plans to graduate and get the heck out of this grocery business.

One more lesson from Fogle's Food City before we move on. A lesson in consolidation and just how **tight the margins** are in food retail. Fogle's, owned by Bobby Fogle in Neese's, South Carolina (home of the best liver mush in the world....if you like that kind of stuff), was supplied by Thomas and Howard. Thomas and Howard, like many voluntary wholesalers (a term used to describe the supplier relationship between the retailer and the wholesaler) had an inherent desire to want to be paid when they shipped goods to retailers like Fogle's. The basis of marketing is exchange, remember? Two parties exchange something of value so that both parties are better off after the transaction. Well, in this case, Fogle's was running out of their side of the exchange equation- the cash side.

Wholesalers exist because small independents, like Fogle's Food City at the time, are not large enough to buy the goods they sell at the best price on their own. They need a wholesaler to link them together and buy for them. In exchange for a fee, the wholesaler buys the goods from the major consumer packaged goods companies at the best bracket price, holds those goods in inventory, and ships them to the retailers when the retailer needs them. Over time, though, independents sometimes run short of cash, cannot pay their supplier, and then either must sell the operation to someone else, go bankrupt, or be bought by their supplier.

Fogle's was eventually bought by Thomas and Howard, became a Giant Food World, then became a furniture store, and is now well- I have no idea what is there. It wasn't the best area of town. The Fogle's Store Manager through most of my time there, Keith, had a saying, "Ain't nothing but a thing". I never was quite sure what he meant by that, but he was a great guy who left every day with the phrase, "I'm going home to have a cold beer." Small independent stores are filled with some of the best people in the industry.

By the time Fogle's became a furniture store, I had moved on to work at BI-LO. My first job? Night stocker. If you have never experienced the "opportunity" to work third shift in any capacity, you haven't missed much. Probably one of the worst jobs ever. I guess I could have been cleaning porta potties on third shift....maybe that would be the worst job ever. Anyway, the big shiny BI-LO was where I was going to call home for the next five to six years. At Fogle's, I had worked in every department from grinding meat to baking doughnuts. These experiences would come in handy at BI-LO. What can you learn at a corporate store like BI-LO? A lot! My Store Manager at the time, Bob, was a gnarly, irascible cuss (this was the south, remember?). And, his attention to detail? Better than anyone I had ever met. This BI-LO, Store 220 in West Columbia, was the largest volume store in the chain for years. What does it take to run the highest volume store in the chain? *A pinpoint attention to detail.*

I was in fear of our store walks each morning, as I had gradually been promoted to running the night stock crew. But, you know, after a while, it became a game- a challenge. I would finish my stocking load, and then walk the aisles before he came in. I was looking for everything he would see. The lesson? I know it's cliché, but *"retail is detail"* is true. The little things count when it comes to running a store. From building a strong team, to setting high standards, to keeping your night crew happy, they would all be formative lessons as I kept moving up the food chain (yes, food pun). I fully appreciated what Bob taught me about how to run a store and how to set your standards higher than all others. Bob eventually died of lung cancer, so one more lesson from Bob- don't smoke. RIP, Bob.

Through various management training programs, through meeting some people I would cherish the rest of my life, through getting off third shift just to go back on a year later, all while earning my Bachelor's of Science degree from the University of South Carolina, I came to fall in love with the food industry. When I graduated, I didn't go looking for the "real job" I had promised myself. I was there. I was hooked.

Fast forward a bit, through stints of becoming one of the youngest Store Managers in the BI-LO chain (my first store- BI-LO 240 in Pineville, North Carolina), to running five stores for BI-LO (240 in Pineville, 242 on Park Road in Charlotte, NC, to 64 on Broad River Road in Columbia, SC to 33 on Beltline Road in Columbia to 270 on Dorchester Road in Charleston, South Carolina), I was forming a skill set that would become a base for the rest of my career.

I am a true believer that you will never be a strong merchant in the corporate office if you've never been an operator in the stores, where you have constant contact with those people handing you money, the customers. If you have not walked in the shoes of those for whom you are building your programs, you have no idea how they are going to be received or even executed. Besides, being an "operations guy" has a ton of credibility when you are eventually at the corporate office. No one ever forgets the nights you spent re-setting the store in Pageland, or the times you helped re-supply Charleston after Hurricane Hugo.

Then came The Partnering Group and the science called Category Management. Previously, the idea was grocery chains should carry a ton of items and let the customers have variety, variety, variety. Along comes Walmart, and the game changed to logistical and assortment efficiency and effectiveness. Then, a funny thing happened on the way to the Forum, the customer decided they wanted to play. In fact, they demanded that the retailer cater to *their* needs, not the other way around. In essence, we had shifted from "marketing to" to "marketing with". The days of "this is what we have, convince them to buy it" were over. Quickly, the era of "what does the customer want, and how can we efficiently and effectively serve them" was taking hold. For more on Category Management, see my book *Category Management Principles*.

As The Partnering Group, and their lively energetic founder, Dr. Brian Harris, were taking over the industry, BI-LO (owned by Ahold at the time) was forming a Category Management team at its headquarters in Mauldin, South Carolina. At the time, I was working on a Masters of Science in Management degree, and fit the criteria of operationally knowledgeable and able to work inside a structured category management department. I said "no", of course. Why would I want to give up a life of being my own boss in the stores, living in Charleston at the time, and doing my own thing 250 miles from headquarters? Besides, one of my favorite people in the industry, Stuart, was my District Manager. Why leave this? I had even started golfing….

Stuart, upon hearing I turned down Ron's (Vice President of Merchandising at the time) offer to come to corporate, sat me down, and basically said I was being an idiot. I loved Stuart's directness…. Not having to be called an idiot twice, I decided to take the job and move to Mauldin, South Carolina. One of the best moves I could have ever made. Stuart was right. To be on the cutting edge of a new science called Category Management was an experience I could never replace. Not only were the fundamentals something I could use the rest of my career, but I ended up teaching Category Management inside the Food Marketing Tracks at Siena College and at the State University of New York (SUNY) at New Paltz, where I formed the curriculum and even wrote the text book (with Dr. Brian Harris).

The Director of Category Management at the time, Mike, was a burly guy with a straight-line focus on what needed to be done to be the best in the

Lesson

industry. I learned a lot from Mike over the years, and still count him as a friend today. Like I said, it's a small industry. Be ethical, stand to your principles, and you will form life-long relationships where you know you both will do what you say, when you say it, no bending the rules. That's how you form relationships.

At the time, I had no idea why Mike spent so much time on the category definition part of the Category Management process. It was so frustrating, let's just get on with it! Guess what I teach today? **The category definition is the most important part of the process!** Do not go quickly through it. The definition determines resources to allocate, guidelines for who is involved and who is not, guardrails for what to include and what to leave out. Mike was right. Thanks, Mike. One more person along the way who set high standards and attention to detail. I'm starting to see a success pattern here.

As the story would unfold, I ended up with an opportunity to join the Fleming Companies as they were changing to Fleming Inc., relocating from Oklahoma City to Dallas, and centralizing the twenty-nine distribution centers from around the country into one Customer Support Center. If there is any place I could branch out and develop leadership skills to catapult me in my career, it was here. If you could shape chaos into order, this was the place for you. Five promotions later, and as the doors closed for the last time, I had run merchandising, convenience stores, tobacco, pet food, and a variety of businesses that would be sizeable stand-alone companies on their own, but were just part of the massive $25 billion company servicing 3,000 stores from coast to coast, including export to the Caribbean as well as a full-line division in Hawaii. Along the way, I am honored to have met fantastic people! I count my years at Fleming as some of the most formative years of my career.

As the doors closed on Fleming, and the company was folded into C&S Wholesale Grocers, Associated Wholesale Grocers, and the customer base fled like cats when you call them, I moved on to Bozzuto's. A family-owned and led company, with a dynamic trio at the top. Their vastly different personalities just kind of worked for that company. The retailers truly appreciate their attention to the independents, IGA appreciates their focus on the brand, and the industry is a better place because of companies like Bozzuto's. Great people and great friends. If a retailer was out of one case of one item and needed it that day, they would drive that item to them. No questions asked. Their relationships with their retailers are as tightly bound as you can get.

Opportunity knocked a few more times before I became a professor. I went to Canada and headed up merchandising and marketing for The North West Company, operating in eleven time zones (including 42 stores above the Arctic Circle) under the banners Cost U Less (Caribbean and South Pacific), Alaska Commercial (in....Alaska), Giant Tiger (southern Canada), Northern Stores (creatively named for the far north of Canada), and North Mart (designed to reflect an enhanced assortment tied onto the same creative "North"). And then, returned to the United States to Price Chopper, in Schenectady, New York, to head merchandising, marketing, loyalty, advertising, health and wellness, etc. All companies with great histories and excellent teammates.

Now, as a Marketing Professor, food is my default. It's where I go when a student wants an elaboration on a concept, it's where I go when someone wants to discuss how an industry can evolve, it's where I go because it is my

14

comfort zone- my "happy place". Just a little history about a cool career in the food industry! Onward!

Introduction

I can't think of a more important industry than the food industry. We feed people! Think of it that way. This industry feeds the world. We keep people alive. There is a higher purpose inside this industry. Food is for celebrations, food is for mourning, food is for weddings, food is for divorces, food keeps us alive. It is the first step on Maslow's Hierarchy of Needs. Everybody's happy....until they get hungry. This is a great industry!

What makes it great? The people. The people who work in this industry are some of the hardest working, down to earth, people in this world. If you don't have the demeanor to want to interact with others, this is not your industry. The esprit du corps is un-paralleled. We work together, we fight against each other, we solve problems together, and we cause problems for each other. And, at the end of the day, we can sit at the bar together and exchange stories like best friends.

This book is about the greatest industry in the world. If you want to be a Food Marketing expert, I'd suggest you roll up your sleeves and start bagging. Collect information from every source possible, new and old, throw everything in the bag, build your base with the heavy items on the bottom, and never stop adding to the bag. You'd be surprised how much you can learn!

First, the future....

Come with me into the future. Into the vast darkness of the unknown. The time? The future. The place? It doesn't matter anymore. All borders have disappeared. Everything is available to everybody. It's a bright new world where distance and accessibility have been eliminated as "hindrances". It's all about utilitarianism and experience, along with a big hit of indulgence and affordability. The "middle of the road" is gone.

Come take a walk with me. Take a walk down Retail Road Future:

Formats are gone. The massive stores were too big to sustain a fickle and contracted economy, so they all shrunk. The office stores had so much fun selling food, they went half and half with food and office supplies. The "dollar only" stores couldn't stand inflation any longer and the packages couldn't get any smaller, so they went to any price point that made sense. The club stores? Well, once everybody started selling goods affordably, the customers couldn't justify paying the membership fees anymore; so, they stopped charging admission. Grocery stores? The middle ground became strewn with retailers trying to offer fresh food fast and the cheapest milk in town. It didn't work. You can't make money with a "labor-heavy" model and the "lowest prices in town". Everybody liked the "other guy's" format, so they all became the same.

Customer lifestyle is the differentiating factor by store. When everything costs the same, the connection must be deeper. So, all retailers picked a lifestyle and catered entirely to that lifestyle. Hunters? Of course, you have your camping equipment, easy-to-prepare food, shelf-stable goods, flash freezing equipment, apparel, and boats all under one roof. Picture it as a Bass Pro Shop with a full assortment of the appropriate food and supplies. Couples with no families? A "no kid" zone of meals that can be prepared in 15 minutes, a store open 24 hours, an online offer that will deliver your goods within an hour anywhere you want it. Think of it as a pizza delivery for all goods, including clothing and accessories. Remember, formats have no borders. It's the lifestyle that matters. Retailers in the future satisfy every single need for a lifestyle. It's a connection that is almost unbreakable. *Specialty retailers*

17

Accessibility of goods is seamless to the customer. They really don't care how you get it to them. They just want it. It's up to you to figure out the logistics. Remember, the stores that cater to all customers are gone by now. You own the lifestyle, you can anticipate demand, you are responsible for a seamless supply chain. Don't bother the customers with the details. As Nike says, "Just Do It."

Cheap and indulgent work together in this society. We want everything as cheap as possible, and love telling our friends about the deals. But, at the same time, we need the latest technological breakthrough gadget, we want decadent cakes, we want to be "first movers" on all new, trendy or "limited time only" items. Yes, it's tough as a retailer; but, it's all about the customer. It's about feeling smart. What should be cheap is cheap, but we all want to treat ourselves as well. Think of it this way: the ingredients should be affordable, and the end product should taste like a million bucks.

There are no borders between digital, social, in-store or real life. The alternate worlds of online have blurred everything to the point where it's all one world. Today's world is like one big mixture of You Tube, Twitch, Twitter, Instagram, and Snapchat. It's about being entertained, being part of a larger society across the globe, and about a borderless existence. As retailers, we had to understand how the next generation was being hard-wired to think of their world in terms of one steady flow of theatre, indulgence, and communication with hundreds at the same time. Experience is the king!

Everyone cares about everything. Yes, it was already brewing about ten years ago, when it became apparent that we could no longer ravage the earth for profits, we could no longer kill off our ozone and expect not to be fried by our own sun, we could no longer lay waste to the same vegetation that provided us with oxygen, we could no longer sit by idly while people were starving in Africa, we could no longer waste 20% of our food and think the planet could sustain a wasteful stewardship, that we could no longer keep eating pesticide-laden foods and expect to have long and healthy lives. The desire for money was subdued by the need to "do good", to be part of the solution, to help Mother Earth survive and thrive for the next thousand years, to be part of one world, one people, one voice. You see, the amount of information flowing at light speed across the globe

18

opened our eyes to the rest of the world, to the needs of the many, the plight of those we previously could ignore, the impact of non-sustainable farming on the soil, the impact of a civilization that was overly "consumerized".

It was an epiphany to an entire generation, and it stuck. The entire population started caring, wanted to only patronize those retailers who had a social conscience, started growing their own food. And it's not just a tagline....it is a real overt desire to be part of the solution, to be a contributor to the good of society. The retailers without a social conscience went out of business five years ago.

The future is not that far from now. In fact, the seeds are already planted and they are being watered feverishly. It's already happening. Formats are blurring, the middle ground is disappearing, customer lifestyle is in the driver's seat, having a social conscience is becoming table stakes. The seeds are sprouting everywhere. You might say the future is already here....

1- Start and End with the Customer

Step one, and ostensibly the most important step: the customer is at the center of everything we do in Food Marketing. It's not the other way around- you don't create a format or offer and convince the customer to see you as a solution to their lives. It's their life, you get to be a part of it if they want you to be part of it. Having said that, there is plenty you can do to ensure you have a better chance than your competition. In this chapter, we will make connections between customer evolution, trends and power, and how that is changing the game- and what you can do about it.

Reality is....you might not make it. The customer has been "Amazon'd", they expect assortment from all over the world available at their fingertips, they'd like food delivered in an hour, and they expect full price transparency. If you cannot come to this realization, it's time to close this book, literally and figuratively. The customer wants to know "What makes you special?" If you cannot wake up every morning and know exactly what makes you special, then you probably aren't. It's okay, maybe the food industry isn't for you. It's a cutthroat, low margin, high turn business where every penny counts.

Understanding you're still reading, then let's make you special. Let's figure this customer out, and then maybe figure out how to "read the tea leaves" and stay ahead of changing trends.

The Generations

You hear so much about the changing of the generations! Baby Boomers to Millennials to Centennials. The "Silent" generation....what a terrible thing to call someone. The thing to remember about generations, is it's just a start. You cannot "bucket" an entire generation into groups, and "market" to them. People are much too individualistic to be thrown into buckets. And, if you hear someone mention Millennials, make them stop! That cohort has grouped 15 years of people together and decided to treat them the same. Don't do it. Avoid bucketing, but *do* look for patterns. Here are a few:

The customers on the "uptrend" in buying power have mostly never seen a life without the internet and a smartphone in their possession. In fact, the Centennials (Gen Z) claim over 95%

New market is technology driven

20

smartphone ownership. It's not "different" to them to have all this power- they've never not had it. Using a phone for a shopping list, using it to look up health attributes of their food, using it to find hot deals, and using it to check your price versus the rest of the world- it's all second nature.

Multicultural is the norm. A striking fact about the changing of the United States population: 21% of those over 75 years old are non-white. 46% of the US 18-21 years old are non-white, including 22% identifying as Hispanic. It is expected 90% of the US population growth the next five years will be coming from non-white. Look at your team. Do you reflect the future?

Health and wellness is here to stay. It's a great trend, and hopefully lasts indefinitely. Looking up calories and ingredients on the smartphone is here and now. Full transparency about what you are putting in your products is crucial. And, if you manufacture goods and/or are a retailer with a strong private label offering, get those bad ingredients out! Why are you waiting to get the high fructose corn syrup out of your drink? You know it's not healthy, they know it's not healthy, so why leave bad ingredients in until the government tells you to take it out? Come on, think customer first!

Big spending is gone. The next generation of shoppers is showing they like multiple shopping trips. Whether it's because of money, or smaller family units, shopping is so much closer to the eating of that food today than at any time in the past! Shrink your store footprint, make it easy to navigate, trim your assortment to simplify decision making, and make sure your pack sizes are manageable. With the urbanization of the population, massive club packs and massive packs of meats are just not who we are. Let the customer know you appreciate their coming in four or five times a week.

Remove chokepoints. Goes with the last one. Checkout free is the future. It's a freight train with no brakes. It shouldn't have any either, the registers have always been the worst part of shopping from a customer point of view. Sorry, Polly running the register and holding conversations with each customer only made the next person in line angry. It's like when the person cutting your hair stops cutting to make a point- keep cutting! I love our conversation, but not at the expense of my time! If you are not able to offer checkout free yet, then go with self-checkout. Here's the mindset you need: self-checkout is actually offering **good** customer service. It's not a lamentable lack of personal interaction, it's getting the customers out of the chokepoint they hate. Look at Walmart, they switched to self-checkout, including using the belts, and do you see a line at Walmart anymore?

"Compare at" is rocking! If you shop TJ Maxx, you know "compare at". It's combining the customer desire to find "deals", to find discounted treasures, and it's giving the customer something to share with their friends. Everyone wants to say, "This is usually $28, and I stole it for $18!" Everyone. This is unabashedly how retail will work going forward- you have got to make the customer look smart to themselves and their friends. Nothing is smarter than getting a good deal. It doesn't matter how much money you have.

Limited Time Only is right there with "compare at". Same type of idea, except this one adds scarcity. Now, instead of getting a discount, the customer will pay a premium just because they also want to share with their friends they got something no one else got. Scarcity works! Tell someone there is a "limit of 6", and they'll buy 6. LTO never fails to awaken the competitive spirit in customers.

Resale is coming to the forefront. It's a sharing economy of Air BnB and Uber and renting jewelry, so it only makes sense resale is on a tear! Go in Plato's Closet, or Goodwill or ThredUp, or even the resale pop ups appearing in Macy's and JC Penney, and it's a trend for next five years at least. Bargain hunting in secondhand clothes is not for those who "need" it anymore, it's for those who want to tell their friends what they found.

Everything is shared. Yes, these trends are all running together. Everything is shared. Great bargains, super finds, LTO's, in-store events....they are immediately shared with friends. Be part of the conversation. #makeeverythingshareable connect 2 social media

Be social. This is where generations are splitting a bit. Facebook isn't cool, but it exists. It's not dead. Instagram is removing likes, so I'm not sure about the future of Instagram. People live for "likes". Snapchat and its filters skew towards a younger generation. And you may want to learn about twitch, if you don't know about it yet. Twitch isn't an uncontrollable muscle spasm anymore, it's a place to watch people game. Yup, and it's hot!

Diets are changing. Vegetarian is huge (around $300B in sales) and growing, pescetarian (no meat, but will eat fish) is not far behind, plant based and vegan are trending as well. Diets have changed based upon health benefits (or harm from what is being avoided) and/or climate and world impacts. (The red meat methane issue has been discussed for years, but has gained steam.)

The environment and social consciousness are top of mind. Yes, these trends tend to piggyback (cowback?) each other. The concern for the environment has escalated, as well as the social consciousness of how you treat your employees, how you treat your suppliers, how you treat people in general- it's all bubbled to the top.

Tell your story. You cannot operate without a story. Just don't do it. You are special for some reason. Tell people about it. Why should they care about you, your products, your store? People want to know you are not a monolithic generic massive corporation. You are run by people and you have a story. Integrate that story into everything you do, and all marketing messages.

Guns, drugs, cannabis, and race. Sounds like a bad joke, doesn't it? The point is, trends and social shifts are happening constantly. You, as a retailer or consumer goods company, need to understand how you fit into the narrative. Gun control and freedom to carry weapons seems like an endless debate in this country. You should have a stance. I'm not going to tell you what it should be. These are emotional debates, with less facts and more rhetoric being spewed by all "sides". The truth is you cannot stand on the sideline. Take a stance. The public will either like it or not. Being neutral is not an option. Stores should take a stand - they'll at least get support on one side

Virtual reality and augmented reality. A trend shift towards gaming and virtual reality is afoot. If you play in that arena, you should embrace the trend. Where a retailer could see major gains, though, is augmented reality; where you take reality and change it in some way. Show the customer how the shirt would fit them, how the product would look in their pantry, how the meal could come together from your ingredients. You can do this right now. I would say, a virtual reality shopping experience of walking your store and placing things in a shopping basket would be pretty cool!

Living alone and unmarried. No, that's not an ad for alcohol, it's reality. People are either waiting to get married, or do not see the point. And divorce rate is at record levels. A single mom or dad, or a person living alone, has a massive shift in their expectations of you versus those with large families. Large families are not the trend. And, included in here is the "sharing economy", or the desire to not own assets, but to rent them or "borrow" (using an Uber is borrowing an asset) them. How that fits into your retail should be part of your strategic discussions. borrowing economy (assets, clothes, etc)

Robots and drones. The trend to either offer kiosks to replace order taking or drones to deliver products has gone from "way out there" bizarre to "hey, that would work". A world of drones dropping off our morning coffee is not far off.

Workforce participation and expectation. The generation coming into the most buying power has seen their parents "work until you die", they've seen people lose their minds over the stock market, they've seen illnesses and diseases because of overwork- and they don't want that. Do not interpret what I am saying as the next generation is lazy. Too many people brand the "next generation" as lazy. It's not that at all. There is always a Bell Curve of over-achieving, being good enough, and being lazy- no matter your generation. That's called being human. The "work till you die" outlook has been replaced with "I want to enjoy and like my life, and make enough money to live well." Enjoying life's experiences isn't being saved for two vacations a year. New work mindset culture shift

Malls are dead. Their death was predicted for years, and it's here. Don't misunderstand mall "traffic" with mall "success". There are people in malls, but they're not buying anything. In fact, malls have kind of become a nice place to walk around when it's too hot or too cold out, and you just want to walk around. Other than those who have not adopted the health and wellness trend, very few people are eating there, very few people are buying anything, and the comedy clubs and bowling alleys and laser tag places are not working. If you are establishing retail locations, best suggestion is to avoid the mall- the customers are.

Private-label

Store brands are cool. Studies show the majority of the population has become so brand non-loyal, they don't care about buying brands. And, if you're in craft beer, you know this- sometimes an established brand is a negative. Store brands are cool, they provide a value, they provide margin rates for retailers, and they encourage store loyalty. Store brands are a winner, and should be cultivated. As you will read later in this book, they can even give promotional retailers a sound base of value offerings for their customers.

Inflation is the only growth you should expect. What I mean by this is do not set your annual budgets to *show growth*. Set your plans to *achieve* growth. Consumer goods grew at 2% last year, but units did not grow. That's called inflation. If you budget inflation, and let all costs increase to that budget, you're stuck raising prices if you cannot achieve unit growth. Go for unit growth. And, make sure all operating statements show both sales and units. If you show sales growth only, and are not increasing tonnage, you are putting yourself out of business. If you are just learning Food Marketing, read this one again. Units drive future success. Inflation falsely covers retailer issues. You must measure units and tonnage! To add one more piece to it, measure sales, units and tonnage as "same store". In other words, year over year, what existed last year versus same this year. It's the best measure of true health of any product or store.

Wealth gaps are real. This is not a shift in the population. Wealth gaps have always existed. They are possibly more pronounced today, or at least more visible. It's a real issue. A company that shows it knows its customer will be seen as a company that cares about its customer. I'm not saying "give everything back", you need profitability to run a company. I am saying, though, care about your customer. If you are seen as helping provide solutions to society's issues, you integrate into your customers' lives. That's a good thing.

Data works. You have point of sale data, you have loyalty card data, you have tons of data. Past purchase behavior tends to predict future behavior. Overlapping purchases by similar groups tends to predict purchase behavior by other similar customers. You *can* be part of the solution for constant refilling (auto-replenish) of commodity items, suggestions for other purchases, making lives easier. For some reason, it seems only Amazon understands this- and Dunnhumby.

Using data to predict future behavior makes analytical workers in the future highly valuable.

cor·les

Cities are the future. Or, adding to that, "smart" cities are the future. Ask a teenager today if they like driving. Interestingly, driving is not important anymore. Kids in the 80's, and before that, were all about getting licenses and getting the "freedom". Today, a city where things can be delivered to you, where you can walk or take public transportation, where all your solutions are within a mile or two- yeah, it's pretty interesting to the next generation coming up in buying power. Translated: have an urban footprint and plan for your stores, and an urban size plan for your products. Offer delivery or "click and collect". It won't be taken up by everybody, but you still need to offer it. Urbanization is a strong trend!

Retailers with expertise sharing space is the future. Target combining with CVS was just the beginning. Kroger and Walgreens, etc. Rather than develop expertise, why not let experts offer that service for your aggregated customers? At some point, Target needs to sub out their food offering to a retailer that knows how to "do food". Think, if you could find a Lidl or Aldi inside a Target? Game changer, right?

Mobile everything. Whatever you offer and whatever you do, it should be seamlessly available on a mobile device. An easy mobile interaction! Not constantly looking for passwords (make them use thumbprint), not constantly asking for credit card information....make it as seamless as walking the store. Seamless mobile is here now, and is a customer expectation.

Winners won't always win and losers won't always lose. Sears was on top of the world, until it wasn't. A&P ruled from coast to coast, until it didn't. TJ Maxx was a bit player, until it came into its own. Walmart was suffering until it grabbed a toehold, and is kicking butt again! Aldi was slowly expanding until Lidl came to the US. Watching those two "up" each other's game is going to be fun to watch! Super companies with worldwide appeal, and proven track records. They'll both be successful. They have the mindset to understand what to do to win.

Winning means taking it from somebody. I apologize for the cold hard truth, but winning means someone will probably lose. The beauty of capitalism! Market share is a zero-sum game. Have the killer mentality and you're going to be a winner!

2- Category Management

You cannot begin to integrate customer changes or product assortment unless you understand how to categorize your store. If you cannot think of your store in categories, you're going to miss out on trends and the evolving customer.

The effort to document the retailer/ supplier relationship with the customer started with Efficient Consumer Response (ECR). ECR was an attempt to clearly define the relationship between those activities performed by retailers and suppliers, and those demands placed upon the retailers by their customers. The function called ECR consists of four strategies of supplier-retailer cooperation that create superior value for the consumer at a lower cost. The four ECR strategies are:

Efficient Replenishment links the consumer, retail store, retailer distribution center, and supplier into an integrated system. Accurate information flows quickly through Electronic Data Interchange (EDI) linkages between trading partners, while products flow with less handling and fewer out of stocks from the supplier's production line into the consumer's basket.

Efficient Promotion refocuses suppliers' promotion activities away from retailer-sponsoring to selling through the consumer. A key aspect of Efficient Promotion is better matching of the promotional product flow to the demand of the consumer, yielding substantial benefits in operations with much less inventory in the system. Another aspect is developing the best mix of consumer-oriented promotions within categories.

Efficient Store Assortment focuses on offering the right assortment to the target consumers. This activity provides the essential starting point for optimum use of store and shelf space. This is the critical link to the consumer. Adopting an effective assortment management approach improves turnover and profit returns per unit of space. The goal of Efficient Store Assortment is to determine the optimal product offering that achieves target consumer fulfillment and enhanced business results for retailers and suppliers.

Efficient Product Introduction addresses the processes of developing and introducing new products that offer a solution to an unfulfilled or only partially fulfilled consumer need. The goal is for suppliers and retailers to develop more consumer-oriented products at lower costs through more cooperative efforts.

It has become clear that the development and management of highly competitive replenishment processes and promotion systems can significantly enhance a retailer's and a supplier's likelihood of success in its marketplace through cost reductions and higher consumer service levels. Despite these efficiency improvements, however, sustainable competitive advantage will also depend upon their ability to market products and services that meet the complex and ever-changing demands of the consumer more effectively. This opportunity is at the heart of Category Management.

Many retailers and suppliers focus their ECR programs only on efficiency improvements (the E of the ECR), where Category Management also integrates the other three more consumer-oriented strategies of ECR. Category Management provides a working process to realize the benefits of each of the four ECR strategies for a category in a framework of supplier-retailer cooperation. Only when Category Management is successfully applied to this extent will retailers and suppliers benefit fully from the promising opportunities of ECR.

Moreover, Category Management's demand-side aspects can enable a retailer and its suppliers to deal with the fact that, when all is said and done, consumers will have a hard time recognizing efficiency changes between trading partners. They will, however, continue to reward those who better meet their shopping needs. This is not to downplay efficiency improvements on the product-supply side. Rather, it acknowledges that, once achieved, these efficiencies will inevitably become the norm for the industry, not a substantial basis for creating competitive advantage in the marketplace.

Category Management is, therefore, a key component for ECR success since it can be a catalyst to changes that enhance both cost savings as well as turnover, profit, and market share growth. Category Management allows a retailer and its suppliers to move concurrently towards capturing important cost savings, while at the same time focusing on more effective, consumer-oriented marketing and merchandising practices. Experience shows that practitioners of Category Management find their greatest benefits in creating consumer demand.

> Definition of a **Category**: Distinct, manageable group of products/services that consumers perceive to be interrelated and/or substitutable in meeting a consumer need.
>
> Definition of **Category Management**: Category Management is a retailer/supplier process of managing categories as strategic business units, producing enhanced business results by focusing on delivering consumer value.
>
> Definition of **Consumer Demand**: Economic principle that describes a consumer's willingness to pay a price for a product or service, holding all other factors constant.

The growing worldwide interest among retailers and suppliers in Category Management has been the result of a set of business conditions that have increasingly challenged many traditional management methods. These conditions have mandated the adoption of, and transition to, more effective and efficient business processes. Increasingly, it is being recognized that many traditional management practices have not produced the desired results. First, some of these practices have impeded the focus on enhancing consumer value as the ultimate basis of profitability and competitive advantage. Second, traditional practices have been based on a view of competition and competitive behavior that has increasingly lost its relevance in today's changing competitive environment.

The business environment that exists today has created a need, as well as an enormous opportunity, for innovative new management approaches. Companies that quickly recognize and act upon the need to change their organizations will emerge as the leaders of the next century. While these realities are present for all industries, they seem particularly relevant for the retailing and consumer goods industries. These industries have always been characterized by rapid change and disastrous outcomes for those organizations that are slow to change. It is encouraging that there appears to be a growing recognition of the need to re-evaluate traditional methods. The willingness to replace these traditional processes with new ideas and approaches is high on the agenda of many of the world's leading retailers and suppliers. Among these ideas and processes is Category Management.

3- Industry Trends Driving Category Management

Several specific industry trends are driving the emergence of Category Management:

- Consumer Changes
- Competitive Pressures
- Economic and Efficiency Considerations
- Information Technology Advancement

Consumer Changes

Category Management represents a method for managing the complex changes that are occurring in consumer needs and shopping behavior. Consumer needs and lifestyles have changed dramatically over the past few decades. With technology at the forefront of the changes, the customers have almost complete transparency in pricing and information. In addition, population growth rates have declined and consumer spending power continues to shrink, impacting at-home food spending. Given these challenges, retailers and suppliers must intensify their efforts to better understand consumer needs and to meet those needs more effectively.

Many retailers and suppliers have a growing interest in understanding the composition of their "loyal consumer base" and in defining the purchasing behavior of loyal consumers. An awareness is growing that failure to recognize and reward customer loyalty can be costly. For retailers, research consistently shows that while the loyal consumer may only account for 20-30% of consumer traffic, this shopper base can account for 60% or more of a retailer's turnover and profit. A similar scenario exists for many manufacturers' brands.

At the core of the Category Management concept is a focus on a better understanding of consumer needs as the basis for retailers' and suppliers' strategies, goals, and work processes. This focus causes a re-evaluation of many current business practices, which have impeded a greater understanding of consumer needs and opportunities. Take two such practices:

⇒ How categories are described.
⇒ How categories are managed in a fragmented manner across departments.

The re-evaluation can be as simple as reviewing the terms that have been used to describe categories. Category descriptors, such as analgesics, cereals and oral care, for example, may have agricultural or manufacturing process significance; but may not have meaning to consumers as they relate these items to their needs.

Consumers shop to satisfy needs, which are more likely to be defined in terms such as pain relief, breakfast food, fresh breath, etc. The use of category descriptors that do not relate in direct ways to how consumers define their needs can cause a lack of connection between how consumers shop and how retailers and suppliers merchandise, market, or promote in attempts to meet consumer needs. Category Management helps identify this lack of connection by emphasizing that consumer-defined needs and their solutions should be at the heart of decisions on how products and categories are marketed.

Among other management practices that have created a gap between consumer needs and how these needs can best be met is the "department" separation of categories. Take the "pizza" category as an example. Traditionally, most retailers have managed this category in several departments. Frozen pizzas are managed as part of the frozen food departments; fresh pizzas are managed as part of the "deli" department and ingredients to "make your own pizza" are part of the grocery department. The starting point for managing any category is to clearly understand the nature of consumer needs in that category. Do consumers define their needs for pizza as "total pizza", or do they separate needs for frozen vs. fresh vs. make your own pizza? If the consumer need is more at the total pizza category, managing this category as three separate businesses, in many cases managed by three different people, will diminish the retailer's ability to meet the consumer's needs through an integrated pizza offering.

Evidence also suggests that when a single category is managed across numerous departments, sales are often traded among the competing components. Increased sales of frozen pizza as a result of a promotion, for example, could merely switch sales away from a retailer's fresh pizzas and "make your own pizza" ingredients.

Category Management draws attention to these kinds of unproductive departmental separations by emphasizing that categories should be defined first and foremost by consumer need and not by departmental separations. Traditional approaches have created some obvious competitive disadvantages for retailers. For example, the current need of supermarket retailers to compete more effectively against the in-roads of "home meal replacement" providers is exacerbated by the barriers that departmentalization has created. Effective responses to these competitive threats require cross-departmental planning. By focusing on consumer needs and solutions, Category Management provides an approach for addressing these issues.

Competitive Pressures
New approaches are also necessary to meet the challenges of today's intense and varied forms of competition. The traditional focus on similar format competition is inadequate to understand and to respond effectively to the emergence of competition from successful alternative formats. New formats employing different methods of competition have seriously eroded the competitive positions of many traditional retailers. The success of these alternative retailer formats, such as hard discounters, specialty "category killers", online-only, and convenience stores has been felt by most traditional retailers. Of the greatest concern is how these formats compete. Their methods are new and require different responses by traditional retailers.

Take the specialty "category killers" as a case in point. This format has successfully entered categories as diverse as coffee, pet food, and supplies, cigarettes, and tobacco, non-alcoholic beverages, bath and personal care products, baby care and prepared meals. Success has come predominantly at the expense of traditional retail formats. This type of competitor focuses on a category, not at a total store level. Specialty retailers identify a category opportunity and exploit it by offering superior consumer value in that category. There is no attempt to compete across a broader base of categories. In some of these categories, the negative impact on the sales of the traditional retailers has been dramatic.

The key point to learn is that management approaches that only focus on competitive differentiation at a total store level, or even a department level, have not been and will not be successful response strategies to this new form of retail competition. Focus must shift to the "category" level and strategies must be carefully devised at that level. It has not proven effective, for example, to compete against pet care specialty "category killers" through the traditional emphasis on one-stop-shopping convenience of large supermarkets, or on lower overall prices. To compete effectively against these new forms of competition, carefully devised and implemented strategies at the category level are essential. This strategy is the essence of the Category Management process. It provides the necessary competitive perspectives, management methods, and tools to meet the challenges of these new category-focused competitive formats.

Suppliers as well are faced with increasing competitive pressures. In addition to the intense competition among manufacturers in increasingly mature categories, the emergence of high quality retailer private label programs has put further pressure on brand market shares. Concurrently, many suppliers are experiencing unprecedented new product failures. It is estimated that 95 percent of all new items introduced each year will fail within twelve months of introduction. As a result, like retailers who are overstocked, many parts of the industry have surplus capacity especially in the utilization of production facilities.

Traditional sources of competitive advantage for suppliers, such as new product development, consumer advertising and trade promotions, have lost impact as supplier competition is increasingly among more equally-resourced companies. New forms of differentiation are needed. These include superior consumer knowledge and expertise and co-marketing programs with trade consumers. Category Management can, and is, providing the platform for the implementation of these new competitive advantage opportunities.

Economic and Efficiency Considerations
Various economic factors also influence the need to adopt new management approaches. The slow-growth economy in recent years, along with low interest rates, has eliminated turnover and profit growth attributed to inflation. Additionally, the stock markets have pressured many companies to improve their financial performance and have heavily scrutinized transactions ranging from leveraged buyouts to new acquisitions to capital requests for additional production facilities or store capacity.

To respond effectively to these economic conditions, retailers and suppliers must operate more efficiently. The birth of the ECR movement has been a direct response to an industry-wide initiative to reduce costs. These initiatives are revealing opportunities and are developing new, more efficient approaches in both supply chain management (efficient replenishment) and demand management areas (efficient assortments, promotions and new product instructions). Category Management can provide the work processes and organizational designs to achieve greater efficiencies in an integrated manner across both demand and supply-side management.

An important outcome of these economic conditions has been, and will continue to be, increasing consolidation in all segments of the industry. The advantages of size, balanced with local connection, can now be leveraged more effectively through the improved technological capabilities that are now possible in areas such as centralized purchasing and direct marketing. The search for improved efficiencies and lower costs will continue, and will probably accelerate the trend towards consolidation. Similar trends will continue in the supplier sector.

Globalization of brands and marketing programs, as well as the global expansion of customers, such as Ahold Delhaize, Carrefour, and Walmart, will promote further supplier consolidation and management focus on opportunities that transcend traditional market boundaries. Management methods that can be applied in a consistent and more productive manner, across broader retailer/supplier geographies will be needed to support this new business environment. The processes and disciplines of Category Management are proving to be an important component of this capability.

Information Technology Advancements

Information Technology Advancements now make it possible for retailers and suppliers to share information and change collective business practices in ways that would have been unrealistic in the past. The growing availability of syndicated markets, loyalty data, consumer panel data, and the move to open systems and client/server technologies has greatly facilitated the adoption of new management approaches in the areas of ECR and Category Management. These advances are significantly increasing the capabilities of retailers and suppliers to obtain, organize, access, analyze and act upon the data required for effective Category Management.

These systems, along with the closing of skill gaps that have traditionally existed across suppliers and retailers, are creating a "common language" based on complementary information. Category Management provides the business processes for effective deployment of these new skills and information sources without neglecting to provide the necessary firewall systems to protect proprietary data and information (especially regarding prices).

The net impact of all these and other changes has been to enable many within the industry to do more with current resources and to refocus on meeting consumer needs for value, variety, and service, as the basis for creating competitive differentiation. Category Management provides a powerful yet "back to basics" approach for meeting these changes in a marketplace, which is more competitive and less forgiving of mistakes than it was in the past. The principles and disciplines of Category Management are a logical step in the evolution of management approaches to confront these challenges. These are not revolutionary new principles or methods. By focusing on a superior understanding of consumer needs, Category Management provides renewed opportunities for meeting consumer needs; and, at the same time, for achieving competitive advantage as well as lower costs through greater work process efficiencies.

4- The Category Management Process

The Category Management business process is a structured, measured set of activities designed to produce a specified output for the trading patterns and their consumers. It implies a strong emphasis on how work is done within and between organizations, in contrast to a singular and exclusive focus on the specific products or services delivered to the consumer.

The Category Management business process is therefore a specific ordering of work activities across time and place, with a beginning, an end, and clearly identified inputs and outputs. It is structured for action. Unless the participants (i.e., retailer and suppliers) can agree on the way work should be structured, it is very difficult to systematically improve, or "operationalize," that work into routine practices within which trading partners do business.

Successful suppliers and retailers must, of course, offer quality products and/or services, and employ productive business processes for producing and selling them. However, cooperative retailer-supplier marketing, product supply and administrative work processes represent major opportunities for improvement. The Category Management process creates a balance between product and process investments, with attention to work activities throughout the total system, from supplier to retailer to consumer.

Finally, although supplier and retailer have separate organizations, different skills and varying roles to play within the Category Management environment, the process itself is and should be the same for both trading partners. Without a common process, the parties seldom develop optimal Category Business Plans. The process becomes both a common language and road map permitting both partners to contribute their unique capabilities for mutual advantage.

There are several distinct characteristics of the best practice Category Management business process. These are:

- The Category Management business process adopts the **consumer's point of view**. It is the structure by which a supplier and retailer do what is necessary to produce value for their consumers. As the consumers are the final arbiters of work process design and ongoing performance, they are represented throughout all phases of the Category Management business process.

- The Category Management business process also has clearly defined **"process owners"**, i.e. individuals with clearly assigned responsibility for design and execution, and for ensuring that consumer, supplier and retailer needs are met.
- The business process provides a **common format and language** for both the retailer and the supplier. If suppliers and retailers follow significantly different processes, much of the value is lost. The process is a powerful form of common language, which links the supplier's and retailer's business objectives for enhanced results and consumer value.
- As emphasized in the previous section, the business process is directed by the retailer's and supplier's corporate and departmental/divisional **strategies**. These strategies guide the decisions required to complete the Category Management business process.
- The business process strongly supports both the development and implementation of **Category Business Plans**. Well-developed business plans, which are poorly executed, do not deliver either consumer value or enhanced business results.
- The business process provides the platform for leveraging supplier and retailer **expertise/resources**.
- The business process stimulates **continuous improvement** through the repetitive refinement of category data and plans. The output of the business process (e.g. the formal, written Category Business Plan) is measured, monitored and refined on a periodic basis.

The eight steps of the Category Business Planning process are illustrated on the following page.

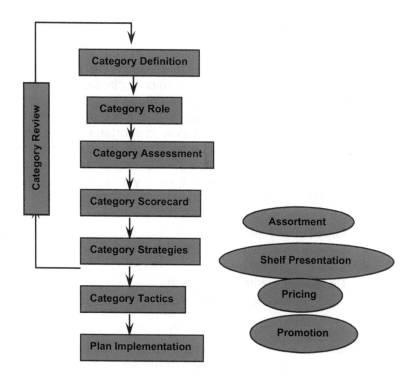

So, that is Category Management in a nutshell (yes, another food pun). But, one word of advice. This is a starting point. Category Management has evolved into Category Marketing, Shopper Marketing, etc. Like I opened this book, you need to form your own ideas on how to be successful. I'm just offering tips.

5- The Category Business Plan

It is crucial to have each category in your store go through the category business planning process. There is no substitute to having a comprehensive plan for each category in your store- from strategic to granular. When categories go through the process, the true meaning of the category to the customer is clarified, new items have designated segments, and trends are caught early and often.

One suggestion on timing of the plan, as well as revisiting each plan- use the six variables below to shorten or lengthen the time between plans. If the variable below is high, the plan timing needs to shorten, as well as revisiting timing. A trendy or new category needs intensity of resource focus even before you see sales results. It's about establishing your store in the eyes of the consumer.

- Emerging trend
- Growth expected
- Limited sources for customers currently
- Lack of information
- Consumer desire to purchase
- Could obtain "first mover" status

Step 1- Category Definition
The Category Definition is the first step in the Category Management process, as it defines the selection of the specific stock-keeping units (SKU's) to be carried in the category, it defines the structure or segmentation of the category, and it clearly states which SKU's will not be carried in the category. One hint, you can work on the Definition and Consumer Decision Tree at the same time. They tend to help clarify each other. It is just as important to state what you are leaving out of your category as what you are leaving in.

Step 2- Category Role
Assigning a role to a category establishes the priority and importance related to the overall business, plus assists in determining allocation of resources, including space, assortment, time, focus, etc. Category roles should reflect the following:

- Desired state- Where do you want to be with this category?
- Consumer-orientation- Is the consumer showing they want you to invest heavily in this category?
- Overall fit- Does this category fit in the store's format?

- Understandable- Once you announce its role, will it be understood by the entire company and its suppliers?

Lastly, when determining role, how important is the category to your target consumer, your format as a retailer, your competitors, and what is the overall outlook? Roles to choose from are: Destination, Preferred, Occasional/Seasonal, and Convenience. At the top, and deserving of the most resources, is the Destination category. As a Destination category, you are committing to:
- Be the primary provider of these products to the target consumer.
- Help define the category in the marketplace.
- Help define the profile of the retailer in the eyes of the target consumer.
- Lead your competitors in turnover, market share, consumer satisfaction, service level, and return on investment.
- Help lead your company's people, systems, and technological development towards achieving the company's mission, goals, and strategies.

All other roles flow from Destination down, in regards to resources and focus. Please remember, not all categories can be Destination. You are actually carrying a "non-efficient" assortment when you determine a category is Destination. If you did that in all categories, you would soon be out of business.

Step 3- Category Assessment
In the assessment stage, you want to obtain, organize, and analyze the information necessary to understand the current performance of the category, and identify areas of greatest opportunity for improved results in turnover, profit, sales, market share, etc. An assessment is a "current snapshot".

Step 4- Category Scorecard
The scorecard determines the target objectives to be set, and collaborated upon, with both the retailer and its suppliers. Set targets by sub-category, work to ascertain market share information, talk to the trade about who is doing the best in the category, etc. Set real stretch goals. "Sell as much as you can" is not a goal.

Additional performance measurements for consumers will consist of household penetration, customer satisfaction, transaction size, and loyalty or repeat purchasing. You need to determine if customers are coming back once they purchase the products a few times. It will also be important to understand the "usage cycle", as in how long does it actually take to use a bottle of drops, etc.

Step 5- Category Strategies
At this step of the process, overall strategic plans are necessary to deliver on the assigned role, and the accompanying category performance targets. Strategies need to be specified between marketing strategies and product supply strategies. One, to make sure you are selling enough, and the other to make sure you are making the desired profit rate (including inventory turnover, shrink control, and inventory dollars on hand).

Strategies encompass the following:
- Traffic Building: Focused on drawing traffic to the store and/or into the aisle or category.
- Turf Protecting: You need to establish this category, then build walls (barriers to entry) around it to keep competitors out. You're here to win, remember!
- Transaction Building: Focused on increasing the size of the average transaction in the category, aisle, or total basket size.
- Excitement Creation: Communicate a sense of urgency or opportunity to the consumer.

For the product supply strategies, you'll need to consider the following:
- Master Data Alignment: This aspect of the process ensures accurate exchange of product, price, and promotional information between the retailer and the supplier. Retailers and suppliers waste too much time on inaccurate data!
- Ordering: Ensuring the right deliveries are triggered at the right time is essential. If you can hook into Continuous Replenishment (CRP), you should; but, be careful, CRP includes an estimate of item movement- which will be difficult to understand as the sales increase.
- Physical Distribution: The physical product flow from manufacturer to retailer, with a focus on higher service levels, ample stock levels, and lower handling and distribution costs.

- Finance: Financial transactions between suppliers, retailers, stores, etc. A focus on error-free invoices, timely payments, and minimal human interaction, is essential.

For the next step, sort your products by strategy:
- Traffic Building: Products with high share, high household penetration, frequent purchase, and are promotion sensitive.
- Turf Protecting: Known price value products, frequently promoted by target competitor.
- Transaction Building: Products with larger transaction size, and premium products.
- Excitement Creation: New products, seasonal products, rapidly growing products.

If you are a supplier or manufacturer, your job is even more difficult. You are, presumably, producing your products to be sold in all retailers. You will need to develop marketing and product supply strategies by retailer format, as each retailer format has a different target customer, different pricing structure, and different brand message. As a reminder, the dominant formats are:
- Mass merchants: Defined by everyday value-orientation, medium SKU assortment breadth, large footprint and 10-25 mile geographic customer draw.
- Traditional/Promotional: Defined by decent everyday value coupled with highly promotional pricing, extensive SKU assortment breadth, medium footprint, and 5-10 mile geographic customer draw.
- Opening Price Point: Defined by the lowest everyday prices, limited assortment, small footprint, and 1-5 mile geographic customer draw.
- Convenience: Defined by competitive prices on key categories coupled with convenience pricing on non-key categories, large assortment in a few key categories coupled with miniscule assortment in other categories, and a convenience geographic customer draw.
- Specialty: Defined by pricing reflecting the specialization in assortment and sourcing, specialized assortment, and large geographic draw with a smaller focused population.

Step 6- Category Tactics

This step identifies the specific actions to implement the strategies, while keeping in mind the category's role. In the Category Tactics step, tactics are developed in Assortment, Pricing, Promotion, and Shelf Presentation. This is probably where you will have the most fun.

For these steps, the following are the considerations, all while keeping in mind your own specific retailer format:

Assortment

In this step, you are balancing the assortment needs of your consumer with the business objectives of the retailer and suppliers. You are also establishing criteria for carrying or deleting SKU's.

The appropriate assortment tactics should only be decided after considering the following factors:

✓ Variety Needs of Target Consumer
  o What does the Consumer Decision Tree indicate?
  o What are the minimum coverage levels for variety to meet consumer needs?
✓ Current Variety Image
  o How does the current variety compare to competition?
  o Who is perceived to be the current category variety leader? Why?
✓ Marketing Strategy
  o What level of variety is consistent with the retailer's overall marketing strategy?
✓ Category Role and Strategies
  o What level of variety is consistent with the category role and strategies?
✓ Cost/Benefit of Different Variety Levels
  o What are the opportunities?
  o How "long" is the tail? (e.g., last 2% of turnover comes from last 20% of SKUs)
  o What is the minimum performance acceptable to carry an item?
  o What is the gain required to offset the cost on inventory, space, and administration?
  o What is variety and what is duplication?
✓ Product Acceptance and Deletion Criteria

44

- o What criteria should be used for accepting and rejecting products given the category role and strategies?
- ✓ Supplier Capabilities
  - o Can category suppliers support tactical decisions?

Pricing
Tactics in this area determine the prices the retailer offers to consumers for the products carried in the category. As with all decisions in all tactical areas, these decisions must be based on the category's role, target performance measures, and category strategies as well as on an understanding of consumer and competitive behavior. The key tactical choices that exist in pricing are:

- ✓ Value Provided to Target Consumer
  - o How important is pricing in the value offered to consumers in this category?
  - o How price sensitive are target consumers?
  - o Which products are the most price-sensitive in the category?
- ✓ Current Price Image
  - o What does the category assessment reveal?
  - o How does the pricing compare to competition?
  - o Who is perceived to be the category price leader? Why?
  - o What are the key price image items of the category?
- ✓ Marketing Strategy
  - o What pricing is consistent with the company's overall pricing and marketing strategy (e.g., high/low, EDLP, etc.)?
- ✓ Category Role and Strategies
  - o What pricing is consistent with the category role and strategies?
- ✓ Cost/Benefit of Various Pricing Options
  - o Will price increase/decrease significantly impact category turnover and profit?
  - o Are private label items priced correctly in relation to supplier-branded products?
  - o How should new items be priced?
  - o What are likely competitor responses to any price changes?

Promotion

Tactics in this area determine the retailer promotions to be offered to the consumer in the category. The promotion tactics define the criteria for using various vehicles (advertised features, displays, sampling, contests, etc.) to promote the components of the category (e.g., segments, brands, SKUs, etc.) to execute the category strategies. Specific promotional tactics are defined, and the final output of this step is a detailed calendar of promotional events linked to the achievement of the category strategies. Promotional tactics play an especially important role in the Category Business Plan because they are the main source of creative selling ideas.

The questions include:
- ✓ Marketing Strategy
  - o What promotions are consistent with the company's overall marketing strategy?
  - o How will the target consumer respond to various promotions?
  - o What is the promotion activity of competitors in this category?
  - o How will competitors respond to various promotions?
  - o What impact does promotion have on the image of the item, category, and retailer?
- ✓ Category Role and Strategies
  - o Which promotions best deliver the assigned role and execute the category strategies?
  - o What criteria are most important for choosing the right promotions?
- ✓ Cost/Benefit of Various Promotions
  - o How well do promotions work in the category? Do they increase turnover? Market share? Profit for the category? How much do they cannibalize existing results?
  - o Does the promotion attract new consumers and do they buy other products as well as the promoted item?
  - o Which promotions build consumer loyalty?
  - o Which promotions create unfavorable purchasing behavior and erode brand and store equity?
  - o What do various promotional options cost? What return on investment does a promotion generate?

Shelf Presentation

Tactics in this area determine how the category will be presented to consumers at the point of sale. Some of the key decisions made in this step are the criteria used for managing shelf space (in the category, sub-categories, segments and SKUs), category location in store and in aisle, category layout, on-shelf service levels (e.g., minimum days of supply, case pack out, etc.), and specific sub-category/ segment and SKU space allocation.

The decisions must also reflect important strategic issues, such as the best location for the category in the store and the best overall flow of products on the shelf. Tactical decisions are extremely important because consumers primarily see the result of Category Management at the shelf level.

These decisions include:
- ✓ Target Consumer
    - o Is the shelf presentation logical and "shoppable" based on the needs and/or wants of the target consumers and how they make purchase decisions in the category (the Consumer Decision Tree)?
- ✓ Competitive Positioning
    - o Does the shelf presentation help highlight key points of competitive differentiation sought by the retailer?
- ✓ Marketing Strategy
    - o Is the desired variety image communicated and reinforced by the shelf presentation?
- ✓ Category Role and Strategies
    - o What shelf presentation is consistent with the category role and strategies?
- ✓ Cost/ Benefit of Various Shelf Presentation Options
    - o How are operational issues considered (e.g. cost of restocking)?
    - o What impact will a location within the store have on category sales and profit?
    - o What impact will a category layout have on category sales and profit?
    - o Does the shelf presentation help the retailer implement its customer service strategy at store level?

Step 7- Plan Implementation

This step in the Category Management process develops a specific implementation schedule and assigns responsibilities for completing all tactical actions. The potential benefits of Category Management lie in the implementation of Category Business Plans. These plans are of little value if they are not implemented, or are implemented poorly.

The key components of plan implementation are:
o Approval Process
o Assigning Responsibilities
o Scheduling

Plan Approval Process
The criteria for approval of a Category Business Plan should include:
- Strategic Fit- Management should be certain that the Category Business Plan is consistent with the company's overall strategy.
- Target Performance Impact- An important aspect of the approval process is to confirm the projected impact of the plan on the category performance targets.
- Resource Allocation- The approval process should "sign-off" on any additional resources requested by the retailer and the supplier, especially if the plan requests additional resources beyond what has already been allocated (e.g., a new type of cooler, more shelf space, more promotion activity, etc.).
- Impact on Other Areas- If the Category Business Plan impacts other functional areas of a retailer's or supplier's business, the approval process must recognize and manage this issue. For example, will the promotional tactics within the plan have any implications for the supplier's marketing function? Will the retailer's store engineering department be impacted by plans to relocate the category within the store? Answers to these types of questions should have been provided in the development of the Category Business Plan, but it is important that management agree to manage these issues as part of the plan approval process.

Assignment of Responsibilities
This step involves assigning each tactical action required in the plan to individuals for execution. Retailers typically assign tasks to the

category manager, senior management and functions throughout their system (e.g., store operation, logistics, information systems and finance).

Suppliers may assign tasks to the account executive, senior management, product supply, information systems, customer service and, frequently, marketing or product development. For example, to implement the assortment tactics, it may be necessary to authorize several new products, discontinue stocking some items, revise the planogram and reset store shelves. The implementation plan will assign each of these tasks to individuals in the supplier's and retailer's organization.

Implementation Scheduling
This step involves the development of timelines and milestones for the tasks, which have been assigned. An essential tool for quality implementation is a detailed implementation calendar. The calendar includes dates for completion of all tactical actions, as well as dates for reviewing plan progress.

Implementation
Success Requirements

- Top management commitment to implementation
- Detailed Implementation Plan
- Involvement of Store Operations
- Category Plans must be "store relevant"
- Review and redesign current implementation processes
- Assign specific responsibility and performance measures at HQ and store levels

Step 8- Category Review
The final step in the Category Management process is to conduct an ongoing review and measurement of the progress of the plan towards the category role and target performance measures, and to modify the plan as appropriate. Category Business Plans are typically annual

plans. Their results should he extensively reviewed annually and less extensive reviews should be conducted at least on a quarterly basis.

Some of the key questions when measuring the category's performance are:

- ✓ How often should the Category Business Plan be evaluated? This will depend upon the category and its role. Destination categories tend to be evaluated more frequently.
- ✓ What role does the retailer play in measuring the category's progress? The supplier? This will depend upon the information capabilities of each party.
- ✓ What format should this measurement reporting follow? A common review format for all plans should be developed to eliminate the confusion and complexity created by having different formats and measures. This format should contain, at a minimum, a comparison of actual vs. target performance levels, an explanation of any variances and actions to be taken to modify the plan's implementation because of these variances.

6- Customer Lifestyle as a Differentiator

It is common in many retailers to use store volume and geography as the primary variables used to set store assortment and layout. I would strongly suggest this practice is misguided and does not maximize a retailer's potential in a market. Yes, pay attention to local items, that is a given. But, I would suggest, lifestyle is a better differentiator for the food retailer. In this framework, we will suggest a method to be utilized that is more intensely focused on customer lifestyles, as exemplified by income, family stage, store brand and organic purchasing behavior than store location and store volume. When used in a food retail setting, the method described in this framework should lead to a more effective and efficient merchandising and promotional system. Results should be seen in lower inventory levels, effective targeting of promotions, and improved sales per store.

Shoppers' age, gender, occupation, education, monthly household income, family size and distance travelled to store have significant association with retail format choice decisions, which will in turn impact food purchase decisions. The choice decisions are also varied among shoppers' demographic attributes. The findings from shoppers' psychographic dimensions like values, lifestyle factors and shopping orientations resulted in segmentation of food and grocery retail consumers into hedonic, utilitarian, autonomous, conventional and socialization type.

To understand how retailers can identify their primary customers, then also optimize the effectiveness of the relationship with their customers, we are looking at how foreign entry modes can be used, even when the retailer is not expanding internationally. In a sense, use the foreign entry mode practices that are already developed as a means of connecting with the customers, *even if only moving from one state to another.* If the existing research can be adapted to the lifestyle trait model, then existing secondary research can provide a blueprint for how a company and its leadership can optimally function in a domestic or global marketplace, while also strengthening its brand umbrella under which all operations will fall. What is the best strategic method for operating in multiple countries, as well as domestically?

In understanding the global consumer, it is suggested that grouping the consumer by lifestyle is more effective than grouping them by any other variable. What has been found, is that regions have various levels of demographics, cohorts, and consumer preferences that can sometimes be assimilated crossing regional borders.

To incorporate the idea that lifestyle usurps the value of geographical grouping, Court, French, McGuire, and Partington suggested following three rules for effective lifestyle marketing:

- **Build a three-dimensional opportunity portfolio-** Create a segmentation scheme based upon the size and nature of clusters of customers who desire specific combinations of functional, process, and relationship benefits.
- **Deliver marketing on a backbone of technology-** Properly develop the technology to "mass-customize" your customer segment offers and use data to effectively spend your marketing funds.
- **Spend your funds where they work the hardest-** Allocate money on the basis of your customers' current and potential profitability - not revenue.

It is highly recommended that food retail companies follow a complete analysis of their touch points, in order to properly align strategies and tactics by lifestyle. This analysis includes:

- **Pre-purchase touch points-** A collection of touch points that significantly influence whether a prospect will place your brand into his or her final purchase consideration set on the way to satisfying their needs.
- **Purchase touch points-** All the touch points that move a customer from consideration of your store to visiting it.
- **Post-purchase touch points-** All the touch points that are leveraged after the sale, including the actual product or service usage, to help reinforce the purchase decision.
- **Influencing touch points-** All the brand touch points that indirectly help to make an impression of the store on its customers and various stakeholders, such as annual reports, analysts' reports, current and past customers, and recruiting materials.

The impact of each of these touch points will vary by state and product. The matrix will need to be set-up by the same: state and product, and will include three customer types: loyal customers, one-time customers, and newer customers. According to Robert Tucker:

- **Do not confuse *your* definition of value with that of your *customers*.** Adding the wrong value is easy to do. When a company is so focused on its own internal processes, it sometimes forgets to ask the customer what he/ she thinks of the company's value offer. Instead of adding something that improves your value offer, you actually add something that takes value away. Interpreting customer needs can be done through customer surveys, focus groups, and one-on-one interviews.
- **Figure out what business you are in.** Intelligent companies do not compete; they out-think and out-innovate the competition by adding unique value. You can only do this by understanding what business you are in. If you sell groceries, you feed people. If you rent cars, you provide transportation; and if you operate movie theatres, you provide an entertaining diversion. Understanding the value you provide to your customers will help with out-of-the-box innovative thinking and value creation.
- **Rethink your customers "highest need".** Sometimes, you can assume the services you provide are supremely important to customers, when they are only part of a combination of the total value you provide. When you are so focused on completing the task at hand, you sometimes forget that the customer would still like to be addressed by name, helped with her groceries, and provided with her "favorite" menu item without being asked. A customer still wants to feel connected and valued while enjoying the service provided.
- **Develop new ways to listen to your customers.** Use mystery shoppers, voluntary blogs, Instagram, Snapchat, Facebook, etcetera, to listen to your customers *where they are talking*. A cold, impersonal "suggestion box" is not nearly as effective as a connectivity-oriented discussion in the customer's preferred forum for communication.
- **Brainstorm unusual ways to add value.** Decrease the number of meetings, deadlines, emergencies and other distractions that keep you from having the "free thinking time" that can lead to innovative/ entrepreneurial methods of providing value to your customers. Environmental scanning,

visiting competitors, etcetera, leads to alternate-view creation that can then be applied to your current and future customers.

- **Figure out the lifespan of your proposed value added service.** Almost all innovation can be copied very quickly and exploited by competitors. Anticipate how long your new idea can last before being copied and de-valued by your competitors.

7- Lifestyle Differentiator Process

In this section, we will review the steps to be taken to cluster the retailer's stores by predominant lifestyle traits, to build cost effective and targeted planograms and distributions, to understand the differences and similarities between groups of current and prospective customers, to develop effective products and promotional distributions by cluster, and to enhance the customer shopping experience. To clearly communicate the actions taken, we will present in step by step order.

Step One: Analyze the current process used to determine ad clusters and promotional allocations. The process involves a prioritization of the following variables: geographic area, store size, number of end caps/ linear feet/ equipment, assumptions about economic conditions, historical patterns, and sales results.

Step Two: To more closely connect with your customers, use a concept developed to allocate merchandise and assortment based upon certain polarizing criteria. Polarizing in the sense that there are specific product characteristics that will show strength only in the absence of the other variables. In this step, the variables are determined to be mutually exclusive based upon loyalty card data.

For this step, we define "clustering" as:
The process of analyzing data and grouping elements that share key characteristics to create usable groups for customer-centric assortment, design, and marketing decisions.
The new method of clustering prioritizes: demographics, key item purchases, lifestyles, economic status, and purchasing behavior. The areas of the business to be impacted, and improved:
1. Planograms and distributions
2. Customer marketing
3. Cluster distributions of promotional merchandise
4. Overall in-store customer experience

Step Three: Take the existing store cluster method and perform the following actions:
- Take actual purchase behavior and customer demographics
- Overlay market demand

- Re-cluster the stores by the previously mentioned variables

Clusters are then developed by three over-arching traits:
- **Lifestyle:** store brand penetration, natural/ organic purchases, opening price point store brand sales, and top tier price point store brand sales
- **Demographics:** % African American, % Hispanic, % Asian, % White, % Low Income, % Middle Income, % High Income, % Families, % Singles, % Couples, and % Transitional
- **Economic Assistance:** Electronic Benefits Transfer (EBT) usage, and Women, Infants, and Children (WIC) usage

Step Four: Upon running the data from the retailer's loyalty card database, you will see a high prevalence of overlap in certain variables. The original variables that show the most overlap, and can be combined were:
- ✓ EBT/Low Income/Opening Price Point Store Brands
- ✓ High Income/ Top Tier Price Point Store Brands
- ✓ African American/ Hispanic/ Asian were combined
- ✓ Natural and Organic

Step Five: The new combinations are re-run against the company's loyalty card purchase data, and the new clusters are: Mainstream, Affluent Diverse, Affluent Mainstream, Affluent Natural/Organic, Diverse Mainstream, Mainstream Natural/Organic, Economically Challenged Diverse, and Economically Challenged Mainstream. From one retailer where this process was performed, Figure 1 shows the correlation coefficients used to determine which variables could be combined, to simplify the clustering.

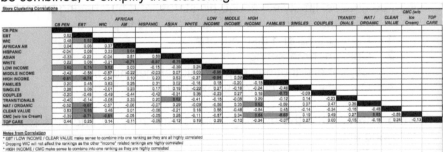

Figure 1: Correlation Between Variables

In Figure 2, we show how the variables were graphically plotted, to understand overlap, and therefore narrow the variables to a manageable number. In this figure, Economically Challenged is the over-arching variable with a correlation between the two clusters, but one group then skewed more towards Diverse and one group of stores skewed more heavily towards Mainstream; which would alter the assortment as well as promotional plan. These graphical representations show the overlap of variables which helped to determine the polarity of the variables, and enable a cluster to be determined to be more like its predominant variable than any of the other variables chosen. This graphical representation is also used in the communication to the stores, to gain buy-in by the operations area of the retailer.

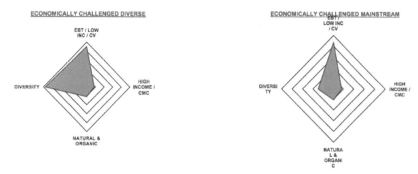

Figure 2: Example of two store clusters with overlap plus differences

Step Six: Once the clusters are completed, the stores are then run against the existing ad zones as a check to see the extent to which the current clustering and promotional allocations match the new clusters. In most retailers where this process has been undertaken, there is a significant mismatch between current allocation groupings and newly formed groupings prioritizing lifestyle.

Step Seven: Based upon this data, begin to enact changes to align with the newly formed clusters. The following are some of the results from the immediate changes made by one retailer.

Initial Results
The initial results from changes made in certain stores were highly favorable:

- ✓ In one store, based upon the new clusters, 16 feet of natural and organic dry grocery were added. Natural and organic sales increased 31.6% in four weeks, margin dollars tripled, and overall store sales increased 2.4%.
- ✓ In one store where the decadent cake set was altered to reflect the new cluster profile, where the customers clearly did not match the new clustering, the results were a drop in shrink from 112% to 76%, and then a further drop in shrink to 40%.
- ✓ In one more broader application of the new clustering, Health and Beauty Care (HBC) pallet distributions were streamlined to match the new clusters. The goal in these actions was to send less inventory to the stores, while maintaining sales; effectively, increasing inventory sell-through. Results were 80% fewer pallets shipped, but 10% more sold, and sell-through tripling from 26% to 71%.
- ✓ In regards to assortment and merchandising, the Frozen Food Category Manager could isolate specific products that needed expansion in certain stores and contraction in other stores.

Next steps include addressing local product acquisition, a continuous refinement of the clusters, a circular analysis and result recommendation loop, a deeper dive into the impact of calling a store Mainstream, and continuing to address the status quo methods in place.

This methodology change in food retail clustering by lifestyle of customers is a first step in a complete understanding of the customers, and how to align the customers with the desire to control inventory shrink, improve inventory productivity, accurately allocate promotional merchandise, and assimilate new stores into new areas of operating, whether domestically or globally. The results reported above are to be taken with caution, and will need further replication to determine if the results from this retailer are applicable to your stores.

Potential considerations for food retailers include:
- ✓ Does your current store clustering has enough data supporting the clusters? The cluster results from this study would be extraordinary if an entire retail chain could realize these results. Each retailer will need to determine "how far off" they are today, before expecting similar results.

✓ Will the operators buy-in to the process? As in any food retailer, the operator buy-in is crucial. Merchandising and Operations are the crucial link to success in any Food Marketing program.

✓ Can the retailer address all the various areas addressed in the study? In this study, the retailer addressed promotional allocations, assortment planograms, pallet distributions, store brand implications, decadent cakes, etc. In one sweeping push, many areas were addressed. If looking at this study as a blueprint for another retailer, the decision would have to be made if the retailer can handle multiple areas for improvement, or if the retailer should focus on one at a time.

8- Store Brands at Everyday Low Price

In this section, we are espousing the idea that store brands can serve a higher purpose for all food retailers. Rather than a margin rate item only, using store brands at everyday low price has shown results for retailers- especially those retailers considered to be "traditional" retailers- where price image may not be a strength.

The food retailing industry has evolved considerably over the last decade. Beginning with the days when clerks would pick your orders from a list at the front of the store, to modern times when the availability of food is seemingly ubiquitous; food retailers have had to shift strategies, re-align tactics, and create new formats- all designed to attract the changing consumer, as well as take sales from other food sellers.

Over time, food retailers divided into formats, with each unique format providing specific utility or differentiators over the other competitors. The balance between price, efficiency, effectiveness, levels of service, utility, convenience, assortment and a multitude of other factors, led to a distinct difference between retailers. The problem, though, occurs when your format is impacted by uncontrollable factors, and you do not make the adjustments to key areas of your business- leading to decreased customer loyalty as well as a dilution in your differentiators. Formats make communication simpler, but they can also be limiting.

First, let's review the various factors leading to the multiple formats we see today in food retail. We will review each of these formats, including their strengths and weaknesses. We will then analyze a study performed at a traditional food retailer attempting to make itself more attractive to customers who may have reasons (the uncontrollable forces) to shop somewhere else. Store brands as everyday low price is developed to offer a specific strategic and tactical response that can be used by traditional food retailers in their battles versus the other formats.

Since 1992, when Walmart, Target, and K-Mart (known as mass merchants) shifted their focus to selling food to increase customer visits, the evolution of the food retail industry has been rapid. Previously to the incursion of mass merchants, food retail stores had been enjoying years of growth through new stores as well as consolidation. Primarily, larger volume and wider geographical reach grocery chains dominated the landscape through aggregated scale and enormous variety. Once the mass merchants began to focus on food as a traffic builder, the food industry began to split into formats: traditional and non-traditional stores (conventional, superstores, drug stores, warehouse stores, supercenters, mass merchants, and convenience). The formats were described earlier in the Category Management section.

The key balancing variables driving the formats are efficiencies in supply chain, promotion, assortment, and focus on certain categories. Non-traditional retailers do not normally offer the same number of products offered in traditional stores, but they tend to focus on certain categories in high volume. Mass merchants, especially, tend to focus tremendous resources towards best in class pricing on certain key categories: household and cleaners, boxed and bagged cereal, pet food, confection, paper towels, bathroom tissue, and dry pasta. In addition, some traditional supermarkets (like Ahold Delhaize's Hannaford and Food Lion) offer a distinct everyday low price format, with high assortment and low everyday pricing. The distinct formats have served each of these retailers well, with customers easily choosing their shopping destinations based upon their knowledge of the formats.

Promotional and Everyday Low Pricing
By dividing into these distinctions of the marketing mix (price, product, place, and promotion), retailers can focus their merchandising staff and marketing message on a singularly effective and efficient model. With economic contraction, though, and subsequent food deflation, all formats began to question their success models and see the other formats as possibly having some traits that will work in other avenues.

In a change from the strict adherence to their formats, Hannaford offers "Wow" promotional pricing, Walmart offers the "action alley" temporary discounts, and even dollar stores (Dollar General, Family Dollar, and Dollar Tree) have begun to increase prices (from only a $1) to add inflation to their sales results. Essentially, the formats are "blurring" their identities in search of improved results in a contracted and deflationary economy.

In traditional operators, promotional (high-low) pricing is a key driver for customer foot traffic each week. Previous research (Huddleston) believed these stores to be more attractive to smaller-basket shoppers, while the same research believed larger-basket shoppers to be attracted to everyday low price operators. Bolton and

Shankar (2003), in a watershed food retail pricing study, suggested retailers construct new and innovative pricing strategies to remain competitive and to stay open for business. This study suggested there is some flexibility in the retail format depending upon local factors, called "customized pricing". The study, as thorough as it was, focused on local pricing, as opposed to a pricing strategy that alters the retailer's "normal" pricing method to compete with formats intruding on their sales growth and customer loyalty.

In the best research leading to the idea various commodities respond differently to promotional versus everyday low pricing, Johnson (2003) described retail pricing as split into two distinct forms: everyday low price and promotional pricing. The study also described pricing in regards to the type of assortment, primarily ranking the assortment by two variables: assortment overlap (redundancy in assortment versus competitors) and assortment lifespan (how quickly a typical assortment loses value or becomes obsolete). This is the first research that may point to the need for traditional food retailers to examine whether they should stay firmly in their "traditional" pricing channel.

Store Brands
It would behoove a food retailer to find a solution for both alternate-format incursions into their business, as well as find a solution that will help build customer loyalty. One of the primary growth strategies employed by food retailers is to grow their store brand program. Growing store brands offers food retailers the following benefits: increased overall category profits, higher gross margin rates, increased bargaining power with suppliers, less risk than focusing on national brands, differentiation versus competitors, store loyalty, and helps attract price-sensitive and deal-oriented customers (Hyman, 2009). The benefits:

- **Increased overall profits in product categories.** Store brands often have higher margin rates, plus show an ability to expand primary demand with price promotion.
- **Gross Margin rates are higher with store brands.** Store brand items are usually lower in cost to the retailer, require less spending on research and development, and store brands are less prone to intra-brand competition.

- **Store brands increase retailer bargaining power with national brand suppliers.** Suppliers will usually react to store brand growth with price concessions.
- **Store brands are less risky than marginal national brands.** The benefit to the retailer is higher with store brand items, due to the higher gross margin rate. Plus, a store brand item that fails does not decrease the competitive leverage of the retailer.
- **Store brands help differentiate retailers from their competitors.** Store brands can be used to create a specific retailer image in a competitive differentiator to competitors. Store brands can be promotional, everyday low priced, treasure hunt-oriented, value-oriented, etc.
- **Store brands boost store loyalty.** Store brands can only be purchased at that specific retailer, so must therefore be repeat purchased at that retailer. Growing a national branded item's loyalty does not promote the exclusivity provided by store brands.
- **Store brands attract price-sensitive and deal-oriented customers.** Whether the retailer is promotional or everyday low price format, store brand items are highly attractive to cost-conscious consumers.

With the blurring of food formats and the need to build customer loyalty, two factors need to be considered by traditional promotional food retailers, to grow and maintain sales momentum and return customers:
- How do we compete against everyday low price operators?
- How do we encourage loyalty from our customers?

The suggestion: If we move the pricing of our store brands program to everyday low price, and then communicate those prices, we will see a sales increase at a higher rate than the national brands versus last year.

9- Store Brands at EDLP Results

The store brands EDLP test was to address the needs for a traditional food retailer to have a viable strategy versus everyday low price operators, without diminishing its identity as a promotional retailer. In addition, the intrinsic benefits that come from store brands growth should increase customer loyalty and repeat visits- ostensibly building a barrier to entry around the retailer versus the competition.

The study aimed to expand the domain of store brands strategies by including a broader sales growth role than is normally found in the branding literature, particularly using store brands as a centerpiece of growth and not solely as a less expensive option to national brands.

Methodology and process:
- The middle tier (or national brand equivalent) store brands items of a major food retailing chain in the United States were changed to an everyday low price.
- The everyday low price was determined as "within a 10% price range of EDLP operators.
- The everyday low prices were highlighted with shelf tags proclaiming the "Everyday Value" of the items.
- The items were featured in the weekly ads and displays at the new everyday low price.

Dependent variables:
The national brand equivalent (NBE) tier of this retailer's store brand program consisted of 1,300 items (in over 40 categories), and is the set of stock-keeping units (sku's) altered for this experiment. The experiment was performed on shelf-stable items only (primarily center store, with no fresh foods departments involved).

Independent variables:
The national brand equivalent items' sales last year, for the same time period, are the independent variables.

Measures:
The sku's with the new everyday low prices were measured versus their sales, same time period, last year- plus measured versus the non-manipulated "non-store brand" sku's versus last year.

Retailer:
This chain of 240 stores returns an annual sales rate on average of US$5.8B, in a highly competitive retail corridor in the United States. Primarily "bricks and mortar" competitors include Stop & Shop, Shop Rite, Shaw's, Walmart, Target, Aldi, Save a Lot, Family Dollar, Dollar General, Dollar Tree, Weis, Wegmans, Tops, Price Rite, and A&P (at the time of the study).

The Results

In the year before, the retailer being studied had been seeing flat comparable store sales (+.05%), with customer count also flat (-.05%). The retailer, being a traditional promotional chain, had seen a distinct difference in customer acquisition and basket size between the beginning weeks of the month and the last two weeks of the month. These differences had a higher delta between them than in previous years. The company's leadership assumption was that the increased government subsidies (food stamps) were driving the influx of business at the beginning of the month (when the subsidies are released to users) and the drop-off was because alternate formats were more attractive when money was tighter.

Both sets of sku's (dependent and independent group) were measured against each other for one full calendar year (13 fiscal periods), plus against total store sales versus last year.

The dependent group of sku's outperformed the independent group as well as the chain sales and profits. The everyday low price sku's performed at a significantly higher rate than the independent group (+8.59% vs. +.20%). Including both groups, the total store brands program grew at +.94%. Total Dry Grocery for the company grew at +.25% during the same time period. The data was then studied by category, to come to some conclusions, or at least some inferences for future use. Essentially, *are there certain products or categories that lend themselves to elicit a stronger response to everyday low price than other categories, or is the sales increase due to the entire private brands offering moving to everyday low price?*

We sorted the categories by volume, with the directive that we should look for whether the largest base volume categories can be impacted by this program, to impact the overall chain sales volume at a higher rate. Looking at the data from a sales volume perspective, we could come to several inferences:

Cold Cereal is a clear winner. Having both the largest sales volume and largest % sales increase, this category showed the highest impact of the program. With the high-low strategy employed by the market leaders like Kellogg's, an everyday low price offering can be a welcome sight for many customers. In this category, we also ended up with three price point groupings ($1, $2, and $3), with many sku's going up in price (i.e. from $1.79 to $2 everyday); so, we built some inflation into the results. Also, cereal lends itself to a more aesthetic "brand block". When all the cereal sku's involved are placed in one block, the packages are bright, vibrant and eye catching.

Bags were winners. We were only able to infer that the snap and seal bags, sandwich bags, 40 count trash bags, and 28 count drawstring bags reacted positively to the changes to everyday pricing. The inference is that the categories which tend to be focus of mass merchants and everyday low price retailers may respond positively to an everyday price. For that argument, we could also include Cold Cereal, Pasta and Dairy products, as these categories also tend to have a strong focus and higher market share in mass merchants.

All "Mass Merchant" categories showed positive results. There was a strong connection between those categories traditionally focused upon by mass merchants and everyday low price food retailers. These categories had extremely strong results in the everyday low price test. In fact, all categories except three (Dry Pasta, Hot Cereal, and Spaghetti Sauce), responded at double or more than the rate of the rest of the group. Large categories like Paper Towels (+13.59%), Yogurt (+10.12%), Cheese (+19.27%), and Bathroom Tissue (+80.75%) show a clear relationship between "everyday use" categories and everyday low prices. Other factors that would need to be taken into consideration in future studies would be commodity fluctuations or other market variables (such as fuel pricing impacts, etc.).

Results prompted program adoption. The results were significant enough for this retailer to adopt the pricing model permanently. It suggests that successful food retailers explore pricing models different from their preferred format to enhance sales growth. The study also suggests a link between traditional "mass merchant categories" (those categories offered at everyday low price in mass merchants- household, paper goods, cereal) and growth through everyday low pricing.

Even considering the various unknowns, we believe we can suggest specific inferences for store brand pricing in highly promotional food retailers. "Mass merchant" categories may show a positive increase in sales through an everyday low price component being added to the marketing mix. Paper Goods, Household, Detergent, and staple everyday categories can benefit from a consistently low price available the entire month on certain sku's. Heavily promoted categories could react favorably to an everyday low price component. In this specific study, Cold Cereal responded extremely well (best in the study) to an everyday low price grouping of sku's being "brand blocked" in the cereal aisle.

In conclusion, there are more positive results that came from this study than negative. Further studies will need to be conducted to ensure a closer link to causation, but the results do seem to suggest a strong correlation or at least an ability to infer possible results.

10- Brand Message

Every food retail company in the world connects in the same way- with their brand. How they go to market, how they engage customers, how they price their products, even how their company can connect on a "higher purpose"- all strategies, tactics, communications, and actions should be centered upon the brand message. Know your brand and you are heading in the right direction. Forget your brand and risk being over-taken by your competition. The world of food retail is tight on margins and heavy on traffic. If you are going to compete, you need an identity.

In reality, your brand message makes things easier for the customer. Whether it's the tagline "Save money, live better" or "Best in Fresh", your brand message confirms to the customer exactly what to expect from you. In turn, your format should reflect your brand, and vice versa. World marketing guru Kevin Lane Keller describes brands in the following manner: "Brands....are a shorthand way for consumers to reduce risk. As life gets more complicated and consumers have less time, the ability of a brand to be a predictable experience is important, in that consumers will automatically return to the same brand."

Hans G. Gueldenberg, previously Chief Executive Officer of Nestle Deutschland AG, described branding as: "Brands are road signs that help people find orientation in the jungle of supply." Brands were further described as "personalities" and a "source of reputation that customers can trust." It was once acceptable to solely provide superior products and distinctive functional benefits. But today's brands must also address process benefits (making transactions between buyers and sellers easier, quicker, and cheaper) as well as relationship benefits (rewarding the willingness of consumers to identify themselves and to reveal their purchasing behavior).

Think of your brand integration into the consumer's mind as a four-step process:

1. **Brand introduction-** Tell them about you, your brand, your store, what they can expect from you.
2. **Brand alignment-** Did your brand or store meet their expectations? Did they walk in looking for everyday low prices and find weekly specials and everyday high prices? Were they looking for limited assortment and find a plethora of items to

satisfy them? Your brand message and store experience need to align.

3. **Brand preference-** Once expectation and experience align, are you now the preferred store or the preferred brand? Will the customer start to drive past competitors to get to you?

4. **Brand advocacy-** The holy grail of branding. Do customers like you so much they cannot understand why everyone isn't shopping there, or buying your products? Do they love you so much, they tell everyone? Think Wegmans. Advocacy is the holy grail of brand connection. Get there and the customers start to do your marketing for you.

The best method to ensure your brand and brand message's customer connection is through brand touch points. All brands have multiple customer touch points. Touch points describe the various interaction points between the brand and the eventual consumer. Defined, a brand touch point is how your brand interacts with, and makes an impression on, customers, employees, and other stakeholders. Every action, tactic and strategy you undertake to reach customers and stakeholders, from advertising to cashiers, is a touch point. Touch points to measure:

1. **Brand awareness and brand recognition-** Direction as to whether the entire marketing mix is effectively getting your brand out to its target audience.

2. **Brand understanding-** Whether potential customers have knowledge about what your brand stands for, the value it provides, and the benefits that can accrue from experiences with your brand.

3. **Brand uniqueness-** Degree of uniqueness that current and potential customers ascribe to your brand, especially as it relates to your adopted point of difference from other brands.

4. **Brand consideration-** Helps make the link between brand preference and the degree to which customers are putting your brand into their final consideration set.

5. **Brand purchase conversion-** Measures the degree to which your brand is put into a final purchase consideration set and your ability to convert that consideration into a sale.

6. **Brand delivery-** Measures whether current and potential customers believe you are delivering upon and fulfilling your brand promise.

7. **Brand satisfaction-** Determines whether the brand lived up to expectations.
8. **Brand advocacy-** Measures and assesses those customers who are considered loyal to your brand and their willingness to put their reputation on the line by recommending your brand.

These facts, coupled with the speed of information, allow a clear opportunity to sink or swim as a brand quickly. Lose the focus on quality and consistency or disappoint one loyal user, and the speed of the internet will pass the word on to thousands of customers within minutes. Reciprocally, live up to your promises, over-deliver on quality and effectiveness, and the speed of the internet becomes your friend. Only retailers and consumer goods companies that clearly understand their brand will survive the next retail evolution.

11- Format as Brand Message

We have described formats a number of times already in this book. In this chapter, we will dive deeper into how the format of your store (or multiple formats, if you choose to operate in that manner) will convey your brand message in a more cohesive or intuitive manner. The way to view it, the customer should be able to walk your store and intuitively "feel" what you are trying to communicate. Inexpensive, fresh, bulk, specialty, organic, etc., is all communicated by what the customer sees. Then, as the customer digs deeper, they then understand how the format comes through in your pricing, assortment, locations, services, etc.

Looking globally, it is interesting to note that North American retailers, due to economies of scale and the ability for "singular format only" retailers (like CVS and Walgreen's) to be successful, primarily trade in one format and one channel, even if under different banners (like Kroger). Western European and other international retailers are more land-locked and dominant in their market area, and must operate in multiple channels to grow.

Tesco has been able to successfully use its brand throughout multiple formats and channels. Now, Carrefour and Walmart are joining the mix of retailers attempting to do the same. When a brand has enough positive equity with consumers, it can transfer this brand equity from format to format. In the case of Carrefour, the company is converting its Champion grocery stores to the Carrefour Market banner. Additionally, all of its smaller, neighborhood stores (Shopi, 8 a Huit, Marche Plus, Proxi, and Sherpa) are being re-branded as Carrefour City in urban areas and Carrefour Contact in rural areas. Wal-Mart has recently added the words "Walmart" to its smaller format. By using a common brand, the synergies of advertising and brand recognition grow exponentially. Sainsbury's and Casino, two other Western European retailers, are also using the same concept. Growth by format:

Hypermarkets and supercenters: These markets are characterized by medium assortment with high levels of inventory on those sku's, passable fresh departments with very little service, everyday low prices, and a large geographical draw.

In these formats, the growth has slowed some in the developed areas (North America and Western Europe), but the format is the preferred growth model for Asia, Central and Eastern

Europe, Africa, and the Middle East. In the Middle East and Africa, the number of hypermarkets is predicted to double in the next ten years. This expansion is mostly fueled by the French retailers Carrefour and Casino. The format's attractiveness is fueled by the ability to offer a one-stop shopping experience and offer the option to consolidate logistical deliveries across geographies. The potential issues with hypermarkets include: fresh and foodservice attractiveness, large square footage to cover fixed expenses when sales are slow, and the discretionary aspect of the non-foods carried in these stores.

China is a primary target for most international retailers. Tesco, Walmart, and Carrefour compete head to head in China, along with the likes of Auchan, Seven & I, AEON, and Casino. Most retailers have used the hypermarket format, with growth increasing five-fold in the last four years. In China, the top thirty grocers represent 605 hypermarkets and superstores, compared to only 125 in 2003. In the next five years, China expects to add an additional 535 hypermarkets, making the total 1,140.

Carrefour is the leader in China currently, namely because the retailer adapted its format to local tastes immediately upon entering the country. In China, the hypermarkets tend to be located in the middle of the cities, rather than the outskirts (like in North America and Western Europe). This proximity to the population causes hypermarkets to be visited two to three times per day by customers, which is not the norm in other parts of the world. Chinese customers usually bike or walk to the stores, which limits their ability to carry large amounts of products home with them. The primary deciding factor for selecting where to shop usually lies in the retailer's ability to offer the freshest and widest array of produce.

Supermarkets and neighborhood stores: These formats are characterized by significant and deep assortment, high service, best quality fresh departments, and moderate everyday pricing- normally complemented by weekly specials or temporary price reductions. Location is a factor in traffic for these formats, so they tend to build out a geography before moving into another area. A range of five to eight miles geographic draw is typical.

Growth of the smaller supermarkets and neighborhood stores will be the highest in North America. Tesco's entry, and subsequent exit, into the United States spurred growth of alternate formats by Wal-Mart, HEB, Albertson's, and most major food retailers. Growth of the supermarket and neighborhood store format in the Middle East and Africa will almost solely be driven by Casino. Casino is the only top thirty operator with a significant presence in the region, especially Sub-Saharan Africa. Casino competes against Shoprite and Pick n Pay in this geography. In Central and Eastern Europe, the supermarket format growth will be primarily driven by Rewe in Russia. Rewe's Billa banner will see growth in Bulgaria, Croatia, Czech Republic, Poland, and Romania. Tesco will lead the expansion in Central Europe and Carrefour will lead the growth in Greece, Poland, and Romania. The supermarket format in Latin America will be driven by Walmart's acquisition of Chilean retailer D&S. Asia and Oceania growth in Australia, Japan, and South Korea will be more controlled.

Walmart's Neighborhood Market format, a direct response to Tesco's Fresh and Easy format (now gone), was designed to be fresh-focused and value-driven. Neighborhood Market's aim is to be more focused on full-service grocery, an in-store kitchen, a bakery, deli, and full-service checkouts. Walmart's Neighborhood Market focused on national brands, while Tesco's Fresh and Easy's sales were made up of 70 percent store brands. Neighborhood Market's pricing is not comparable to a regular Walmart store, since it reflects the increased costs of fresh in-store foods; but they are still competitively priced on the staples of bread, milk, butter, bananas, and eggs. Neighborhood Market is not a major driver for Walmart, as online is seen to have more upside sales potential.

In late 2008, Woolworth's launched a new fresh-focused format in Australia. These stores, named Thomas Dux, are approximately 500 square meters, half of which is focused on fresh meat, fruit, dairy, bread, and an extended dairy. There are 3,000 items in the grocery assortment, and the format is designed to be the opposite of a "normal" Woolworth's store. The feel is supposed to be "homey", with the staff sampling the fruit themselves, warm lighting, and merchandising in a "product first" mentality.

Discount stores: The discount store format is based upon a limited range of products sold in smaller stores. In these stores, you expect no service, only one or two choices in each commodity, a store on every corner- or at least high density in low income areas. These stores are resistant to, if not helped by, recessionary times. As the economy has worsened, the discount store format has gained in popularity.

Discount stores dominate the Western Europe landscape. Where they number in the thousands in the rest of the world's operating areas (2,000 in the United States), discount stores number around 25,000 in Western Europe, and are expected to grow by another 9,000 in Western Europe alone in the next five years. Central and Eastern Europe are also growing at a quicker rate (14%) than the rest of the world. Europe is the "home turf" for discount stores, being led by Aldi and Schwarz Group's Lidl. In 2008, Lidl had more stores than Aldi in Western Europe for the first time ever (although Aldi still had a larger sales turnover). The third ranking operator of discount stores in Europe is Carrefour, which runs their discount stores under the banners of Ed, Dia, and Minipreco. The fourth largest operator is Edeka, which operates Netto and recently acquired Plus from Tengelmann.

With Western Europe already having high penetration of the discount format, the growth of the format is going to come from the United Kingdom, Ireland, Spain, Portugal, and Switzerland. Germany, the leader in this format with 11,000 stores, still expects the number to climb to 15,000 in the next five years, as Aldi is attacked by Lidl, Edeka's Netto, and Rewe Group's Penny. Central and Eastern Europe will see the natural geographical expansion of the format, fueled by Schwarz's Lidl, Rewe Group's Penny, Aldi, Carrefour, Ahold, Casino, Auchan, and Delhaize Group. Central and Eastern Europe were hit extremely hard by the economic downturn, and are the most receptive to this format.

North America is certainly also regarded as fertile ground for the advancement of the discount format. A format focusing on smaller sized stores, lower costs, lower prices, and ease of shopping is poised to do well in the United States. The major obstacle faced by the discount format is the fact that they have not been widely accepted by Americans. The American public is relatively spoiled by the vast array of products available inside grocery stores, coupled with great service. The discount format is limited assortment and low service. Also fighting the discount store advance is the fact that most of the world's largest brands were formed in the United States. The discount format, as we know it today, is focused on chain-specific store brands or "off brands". Store brand acceptance is not nearly as wide in the United States as it is in the rest of the world. In fact, it took Aldi more than thirty years to top the 1,000 store mark in the United States.

Aldi expects to open 100 stores per year, especially as it fights off an incursion from Lidl. The discount format which is focused upon dollar stores is showing tremendous growth, though. These stores, led by Dollar General, Family Dollar Stores, and Dollar Tree, number in the 5,000 to 20,000 stores each. As these stores expand their food offerings, the increased traffic multiplied by the sheer number of stores, makes this format a venerable competitor.

Internationally, the discount store format is supported by the likes of Walmart and Carrefour, with 357 and 737 stores each, respectively. Carrefour's Dia stores are found in Argentina and Brazil, while Walmart's D&S and Sam's have been focusing on other parts of Latin America. Casino also operates over 100 stores in Latin America. In Asia and Oceania, discount stores are expected to see growth in the 8% range, the second highest outside of Europe and much faster than North America. Carrefour is leading this expansion, with a strong presence in Turkey and China. AEON and Aldi are also very strong in the Asia and Oceania region; Aldi in Australia and AEON in Japan.

The discount format is well-received in Asia and Oceania, and growth will continue at a rapid pace. Aldi expects to double its store numbers in the next five years. The overall leader in this region, though, is Turkish discount operator BIM with over 2,200 stores in the region. The second largest network is run by LAWSON in Japan. In Africa and the Middle East, there is very little growth in the discount format expected in the next five years. Only Casino operates in the area, and it is only a handful of stores. Shoprite operates over 100 stores in South African markets, GSL is showing strong growth in Saudi Arabia, and BIM entered Morocco in 2009.

Cash and carries and warehouse clubs: The format of cash and carries and warehouse clubs is a high growth format in Asia and Oceania. These stores primarily focus on supplying the large number of independent stores, serving as their supplier and warehouse. The number of cash and carries operated by the top thirty is expected to double in Asia and Oceania in the next five years. The world's largest cash and carry operator is Metro. Metro was one of the first retailers to enter India, and is expanding into Pakistan and Kazakhstan. The future growth will be driven by Wal-Mart, Tesco, Carrefour, and Costco. The Middle Eastern and African region is also set to experience heavy growth, primarily spurred by Metro's entry into the area.

In Central and Eastern Europe, growth will be driven by Metro. This growth will be seen heavily in Russia, Poland, and the Ukraine. Western Europe is not as fertile for the expansion of cash and carries, as the available land is scarce. Expansion will be seen by Metro and Rewe, with the potential that Costco will enter the Irish market in the future. Brazil and Mexico are prime expansion spots for cash and carries, driven by Walmart's Maxxi Atacado chain in Brazil, Casino's Assai chain in Brazil, and Wal-Mart's Sam's Club and Costco in Mexico. The North American market is the home to the most warehouse clubs, with over 2,000. Wal-Mart's Sam's Club has the most number of stores, but Costco leads the market in sales turnover.

Costco has just recently entered the Australian market, with its first store in Melbourne's Docklands. The Dockland's outlet was chosen due to its proximity to small and medium businesses, growing population, and close distance to freeways and public transportation. The store sizes in Australia will average in size around 14,000 square meters. Approximately 40% of the floor space is dedicated to food, with the rest allocated to general merchandise.

Convenience and forecourt formats: The convenience and forecourt formats are expected to grow by 3.4% in the next five years. Central and Eastern Europe are set for the highest growth rate, albeit from a small base, due to the expansion of Tesco's adding new convenience stores in the Czech Republic and Hungary. The growth in Poland will come from Carrefour's chain launched in 2007 called 5 Minut. Through the Latin American region, Brazil and Colombia will see the most growth from the top thirty grocers. Growth will be in the 6.6% range, fueled by Carrefour and Casino's Carrefour Express and Extra Facil stores, respectively.

In Western Europe, Asia, and North America, retailers use convenience stores to fill in gaps that cannot be satisfied by other formats. These formats also offer the ability to hone their skills in ready to eat meals and top-up (or fill-in) shopping. Seven and I dominates North America and Asia with the 7-Eleven brand. Throughout Asia, Tesco will be driving growth with its convenience stores in China, Japan, South Korea, Thailand, and Turkey. Most stores attempt to complement their food and other assorted goods with an offering of gasoline. The convenience store format is not expected to see much growth in Africa and the Middle East.

Casino is looking to expand from its current base, and has identified the convenience store format as a desirable growth engine. The convenience format for Casino is represented by the banners Petit Casino, SPAR, Vival, and Monop. In early 2009, Casino announced the launching of Chez Jean. This partnership with Relay is a hybrid between a coffee shop and a grocery store. The assortment includes coffee, groceries, fresh bread, flowers, newspapers, tickets and lottery tickets. The format also offers foodservice, Wi-Fi, mobile recharging stations, and clean restrooms. The total selling area equates to 380 square meters.

The Chez Jean stores offer foodservice based upon the time of day. In the morning, the service counter is called "Reveil" (wake up), offering bakery items and coffee. During lunch time, the same counter switches to "Ca gargouille" (rumbling tummy), and sells sandwiches, desserts, and beverages. During the dinner hours, the counter switches to "SOS frigo vide" (SOS empty fridge), and offers salads, cooked meals, and desserts. Groceries are supplied by Casino, and offer a much more consolidated assortment than regular convenience stores. The grocery offering includes yogurts, frozen foods, mineral water, biscuits, wines, champagne, fruit, sushi, and beauty products. Surrounding this assortment, there is an offering of newspapers, magazines, and novels.

Drugstore and pharmacy formats: The drugstore and pharmacy channel will have a much slower expansion than other channels in the next five years. The channel is not a priority for most of the top thirty grocers. There is very little internationalization of drugstore and pharmacy retailers. AEON's Welcia only operates in Japan. Walgreens, CVS, and Rite Aid operate primarily in North America. Walgreens and Boots formed an alliance in 2014, which is one of the first major steps into a globalized platform for pharmacy and drug stores. Although store count growth will be slow, the sales growth should be brisk. The aging population, addition and expansion of grocery assortment, and the new freedom of some of the pharmacy markets in Germany and Scandinavia, should help this format grow at over 2% in the next five years. The fact that the channel is relatively insulated from the economic downturn, due to the non-discretionary aspect of what it sells, should help maintain and encourage growth.

Fueling growth internationally will be AEON's Welcia network of stores, accounting for all the drugstores and pharmacies in Asia and Oceania from top thirty grocers; and Australia's Woolworth's, rumored to be looking to acquire Australian Pharmaceutical Industries (operating 500 drugstores and pharmacies in Australia).

In North America, Walgreens, CVS, and Rite Aid continue their decent store number expansions, with Rite Aid a far distant third place. Walgreens alone plans to open 500 net new stores in the next five years, in addition to growing its alliance platform with Boots. CVS acquired the 500 store Long's Drugs chain and has opened a new format called Beauty 360, while also focusing on in-store health clinics, etc. CVS has made "whole health" a priority in its stores, in addition to offering the longest receipts in the world....

With a revised pharmaceutical law enacted in Japan in 2009, AEON's expansion will be centered upon drugstores and pharmacies in the country. The pressure for health care reform and the increased promotion of self-medication, will drive the drugstore format. To expand, AEON has taken minority stakes in regional drugstore chains like CFS. Welcia now has a drugstore alliance of more than 1,700 stores, coming from nine regional drug chains.

Walmart plans to offer 400 in-store health clinics in the next five years. There are currently 36 locations, using "The Clinic at Walmart" as the brand. The first clinics opened in April, 2008 in Atlanta, and they are co-branded with local hospitals. The average visit costs a customer from $50 to $65.

Each of these formats described above has positive and negative aspects to their development, primarily focused upon each of the various global challenges that differ by region. Where new small-box supermarket formats are driving the competition versus convenience stores, improvements in their fresh offerings are making the convenience format stronger. As drugstores are relatively recession-resistant, so are the dollar stores, which are selling the same non-drug items as the pharmacies. And, as hypermarkets are the strongest growth format in Asia and Oceania, they are relatively stable in North America. Each of the major top thirty chains is using the multi-format approach to be able to ensure they have a response for whichever market they would like to enter and whether or not the economy is improving or disintegrating. Land, and its scarcity or propensity, is a key variable in deciding upon the appropriate formats to use by country. As well, the government always plays a role in whether or not the economics inside the country are ripe for retail growth or are limited by governmental factors.

The importance of being able to cater to local needs and nuances cannot be passed over by any of the major retailers. An inner-city retail shopping experience in Japan is going to differ greatly from an inner-city experience in Detroit. The fresh food offering in a convenience format in Copenhagen will differ greatly from the local customer needs for food service in Moscow. On top of that, the needs of the customers in the morning will differ from the needs at lunch, or at dinner, or at midnight. The strong retailers understand these unique variables in operating globally, and offer the multi-tier formats to remain strong.

The strategic designs of each of the global retailers centers very closely to the same operating methods as the global consumer good companies. Localization is the key to success, with multiple formats used as the answer to convey a brand image to as many customers as possible, while still fitting the store format into the desired locations.

12- Rethinking Your Brand

The following is an example of how one retailer looked at their brand, worked to determine how the customers saw them and their offer, and built a plan to be customer-oriented for the next generation of shoppers. A retailer or consumer goods company must know itself first, before presenting itself or its services and goods to the food retailing environment. Knowing its identity will ensure that, during the marketing operations, a company will not lose its core identity as it grapples with the variables that present themselves.

Food Seller A (name changed to protect the innocent), a retailer of US$ 8.8 billion in retail sales in the southeast United States, set out to change its identity in relation to its customer base and future desired market and branding position. The project was named "Building the Food Seller A Brand of the Future on the Best of our Past." In the following, we will describe the steps taken by Food Seller A in identifying the strength of its current brand, the proposed brand, and a roadmap for solidifying the brand presence in the eyes of its customers.

The first move was to establish the "Eight Steps to Success":

1. Establish current Food Seller A image
2. Define vision of the future
3. Establish mission
4. Define customer segments and core customer focus
5. Establish brand personality and character
6. Brand essence
7. Brand identity
8. Put in place pillars of success

Step One- Establish Current Food Seller A image
  ➤ Fundamental strengths to build upon
  ➤ Reflection of information, data, insights and collected to date in research
  ➤ Food Seller A points of parity and points of difference
  ➤ Focus and leverage unique points of difference

As the initial activity in this section, a Strengths, Weaknesses, Opportunities, and Threats (SWOT) analysis was performed. One lesson in business, you will never escape the SWOT:

- ➢ Strengths: Strong value image of price and quality, quality and selection of fresh foods, promotional and store excitement, strong merchandising and purchasing power, values of the company and people, Family-owned way of life, and the ability to act like a large chain while staying trim and nimble.
- ➢ Weaknesses: Lack of defined strategy for the future, no overall brand look or feel, trying to be all things to all people, training and staff issues, store layout and flow, in-store confusion, cleanliness, and lack of overall shopping and buying emotional experience.
- ➢ Opportunities: Support customers' needs to save time and money and make it easier for them to shop, help make the shopping and buying experience more enjoyable and more emotional, differentiate from the competition by providing added services in fresh, be the "go to" place for the target customers' food needs, and continue to strengthen the value image.
- ➢ Threats: Threats of unknown in the economy and competition, lower customer spending power, rising costs, lower customer optimism and confidence, strong and growing emphasis on price, major competition moving towards "everyday low price", competition focusing on "easy shop", and a growing list of international competition.

Also in Step One, the major competitor strengths and weaknesses were determined:
- ➢ Food Seller B:
  - ○ Strengths: Utilitarian approach succeeds with customers who want a simplified shopping experience, everyday low pricing, store layouts, demonstrated leadership in natural and organics.
  - ○ Weaknesses: Boring stores, weekly ads, no shopper card.
- ➢ Food Seller C:
  - ○ Strengths: Strong health and beauty care program, clean stores, and friendly store layout.
  - ○ Weaknesses: Continual shifts in pricing strategies.
- ➢ Food Seller D:
  - ○ Strengths: Reputation, execution excellence, solutions-oriented approach to customers' needs,

staff, everyday low pricing, fresh quality and execution, significant store brand program.
  - o Weaknesses: Size of stores may not be for everyone, limited variety in the center of the store, and price perception.
- ➢ Food Seller E:
  - o Strengths: one-stop shopping, low price perception, awareness and repositioning of their brand, financial clout.
  - o Weaknesses: Size of stores, in-store experience, staff knowledge, fresh departments.

Step Two- Define Vision of Future, where the Brand aspires to be
- ➢ Now: Middle of the pack
- ➢ Future (three years): Leader in shopping experience
- ➢ Future (five years): Store of choice in each market, with core customer versus core competitor

In this section, it was decided that market leadership is assumed to be "holy ground." Top of mind leadership is the goal, and one dominant idea will connect with each customer.

Step Three- Establish Mission
- ➢ Now: Best in Fresh and Value
- ➢ Future (three years): Excitement in the shopping experience. Food Seller A wants to be the first choice for basics plus to be easy to shop, attractive and exciting, and offer helpful and informed service.
- ➢ Future (five years): The customer resource. Food Seller A wants to be the store of choice known for providing helpful people and tools to improve the lives of consumers by continuously satisfying the family's food needs. Food Seller A wants to establish strong customer relationships with established consumer resources.

Step Four- Define Customer Segments and Core Customer Focus
Jeanine: Confident traditionalist on a budget, 12 percent of households, average household spend is US$ 205 on groceries every two weeks, thinks meal planning and preparation is important, does not spend a lot of money on groceries.

Jeanine's preferred store attributes:

- ➢ Quality service in the fresh food department
- ➢ Freshness and quality of fruits and vegetables
- ➢ Aisles that are kept clear
- ➢ The availability of the butcher in the meat department
- ➢ Having the weekly flyer and newspaper ads
- ➢ Price of advertised specials
- ➢ Selection of products for holidays and special occasions

Heidi: Affluent experimenter, 16 percent of households, average household spend is US$ 252 on groceries every two weeks, loves to plan meals and cook for her family both every day and on special occasions, does not stick to a budget, loves to experiment with cooking and considers herself a gourmet cook, does not clip coupons.

Heidi's preferred store attributes:
- ➢ Quality service in the fresh food department
- ➢ Someone is available to answer questions or help her find something
- ➢ Quantity of sale items in stock
- ➢ Having the weekly ad flyer
- ➢ Wide aisles
- ➢ Having specialty cheeses

Lily: Enthusiastic traditionalist, 14 percent of households, average household spend is US$ 234 on groceries every two weeks, enjoys cooking, particularly enjoys cooking for special events and on weekends, meals tend to be traditional, does not plan menus, does not budget for grocery shopping, wings it, does not read ad flyers, does not clip coupons.

Lily's preferred store attributes:
- ➢ Having a frequent shopper card that has many benefits
- ➢ Having a butcher available in the meat department
- ➢ Having a selection of private label or store brands
- ➢ Having products for holidays and special occasions

Shared attributes for Jeanine, Heidi, and Lily:
- ➢ Essential resource to help satisfy my family's food needs
- ➢ Quality of service in the fresh food departments
- ➢ Quantity of sale items in stock

- ➢ Aisles are kept clear
- ➢ Availability of a butcher in the meat department
- ➢ Having a weekly ad flyer and shopper loyalty card
- ➢ Selection of products for holidays and special occasions
- ➢ Price on advertised specials
- ➢ Prices are clearly identified
- ➢ Having wide aisles
- ➢ Selection of specialty cheeses

Step Five- Brand Personality and Character

Food Seller A current self-perception: Down to Earth, grounded, competitive, reliable, and trustworthy

Food Seller A future self-perception: Friendly, engaging, inspiring, exciting, and trustworthy

Personality
- ➢ Outward face of the Food Seller A brand expressed in human terms
- ➢ Personality helps the brand come to life and makes it accessible and touchable
- ➢ Helps to differentiate Food Seller A from the competitors

Character
- ➢ Inward, internal values of the Food Seller A brand and its culture
- ➢ Company's commitment made to management, staff, customers, supporters, expressed in each person's own words
- ➢ Customer-focused, family-oriented, ethical, hard working, passionate, team-oriented, community-minded, trusting, respectful, and proud

Step Six- Brand Essence

Market leadership is the "holy ground":
- ➢ For the most part, people remember one thing
- ➢ Top of mind leadership is Food Seller A's goal
- ➢ One dominant idea to become great

Brand essence:
- ➢ One idea/ word that we want to own in our customer's mind
- ➢ Simple, easily understood and valued
- ➢ Not a little about a lot, but a lot about a little

- ➤ Helpful- improving lives through our goods, services, and relationships
- ➤ Approachable, responsive, knowledgeable, engaging, exciting, convenient, friendly, team oriented, efficient, save time and money

Step Seven- Brand Identity
- ➤ What is the internal DNA of the brand?
- ➤ It is what we get up every day to accomplish beyond our functions.
- ➤ It is who we are: real, authentic, ingrained in our being.
- ➤ Does it come out of the bedrock of the founder's set of shared beliefs?
- ➤ It reflects actions more than words.
- ➤ Does it have a higher focus or noble cause?
- ➤ Are we the customer's hero by providing a more enjoyable food experience, by succeeding in meeting various roles, by reducing stress, by providing value and quality prices, by making the shopping experience more fun, by saving the consumer time, by inspiring ideas, by taking care of the family and food needs, and by helping provide special moments?

Step Eight- Pillars of Success
High-level strategic initiatives to guide and direct each function's tactical and business plans.

Operations
- ➤ Develop service culture; both bottom up and top down
- ➤ Define store experience (service) from customer's point of view; guardrails for managers and associates
- ➤ Empower management to execute programs and hold them accountable with guardrails
- ➤ Develop and promote the right skills and attitudes for success among management and staff. Replace the people who do not fit the culture.
- ➤ Create a total service model for the entire store
- ➤ Manage total experience versus functional silos to create a holistic experience

Merchandising
> Establish focus on core customer segments among merchants
> Use solutions-based merchandising to meet customers' needs and wants
> Creating news: items, displays, deals, WOW deals
> Build in-store celebrations around products
> Simplify- what should be rationalized?
> Provide cross functional teams to deal with issues and opportunities
> Focus on corporate brands

Marketing
> Develop clear brand identity for all stakeholders (customers, associates, trade partners)
> Communicate internally with holistic approach to entire Food Seller A organization
> Support internal branding with how's and why's
> Communicate externally to defined core customers only after it is understood and accepted internally
> Combination of traditional and new media integration into everything, every touch point
> Act as the gatekeepers across all functional areas of the company

Next Steps (Developed after the eight-step branding and identity project was completed)

These steps were identified as:
> Support and buy-in of the brand team and senior team
> Set corporate pillars of success to align the organization
> Bring the brand to life with words (brand promise) and visuals
> Develop internal branding plan to build on best practices- if you cannot measure it, you cannot manage it
> Develop and detail internal and external communication plan
> Develop a launch plan, with team, timing, and budgets
> Use a brand team to kick start the brand process
> Use as context a set of guardrails for development and detailing of the corporate business plan: financial, human resources, people, real estate.

➤ Annual tracking of brand equity: financial, customer, performance; a total scorecard

The above example of Food Seller A is one salient method of establishing a brand's core identity that can be communicated properly, quickly, and effectively to all associates. The process states succinctly that the associates must know the identity before the public can learn the identity.

13- Recommendations

Overall, operating in the food industry is exciting and offers so much opportunity to passionately connect with customers, offer a differentiated in-store experience, and constantly reaffirm "what makes you special". This chapter is designed as a roadmap to use as a plan for food marketing retailers and consumer goods companies. From Robert Tucker:

➢ Don't confuse your definition of value with that of your customers. Adding the wrong value is easy to do. When a company is so focused on its own internal processes, it sometimes forgets to ask the customer what he/ she thinks of the company's value offer. Instead of adding something that improves your value offer, you add something that takes value away. Interpreting customer needs can be done through customer surveys, focus groups, and one-on-one interviews.

➢ Figure out what business you are in. Intelligent companies do not compete; they out-think and out-innovate the competition by adding unique value. You can only do this by understanding what business you are in. If you sell groceries, you feed people. If you rent cars, you provide transportation; and if you operate movie theatres, you provide an entertaining diversion. Understanding the value you provide to your customers will help with out-of-the-box innovative thinking and value creation.

➢ Rethink your customers "highest need". Sometimes, you can assume the services you provide are supremely important to customers, when they are only part of an aggregation of the total value you provide. When you are so focused on completing the task at hand, you sometimes forget that the customer would still like to be addressed by name, helped with her groceries, and provided with her "favorite" menu item without being asked. A customer still wants to feel connected and valued while enjoying the service provided.

➢ Develop new ways to listen to your customers. Use mystery shoppers, voluntary blogs, YouTube, Facebook, etc. to listen to your customers where they are talking. A cold, impersonal "suggestion box" is not nearly as effective as a connectivity-oriented discussion in the customer's preferred forum for communication.

➢ Brainstorm unusual ways to add value. Decrease the number of meetings, deadlines, emergencies and other distractions that keep you from having the "free thinking time" that can lead to innovative/ entrepreneurial methods of providing value to your customers. Environmental scanning, visiting competitors, etc. leads to alternate-view creation that can then be applied to your current and future customers.

➤ Figure out the lifespan of your proposed value added service. Almost all innovation can be copied very quickly and exploited by competitors. Anticipate how long your new idea can last before being copied and de-valued by your competitors.

As with businesses which only operate in one country, product connectivity in foreign countries is under the same stress. Michael Porter describes the essence of strategy formulation as "coping with competition, and that competition comes not simply from direct competitors, but from the underlying economics of the industry.". Porter's work portrayed "five forces" affecting product viability, company profitability, and customer connectivity. These five forces are as follows:

➤ Character among rival competitors: The rivalry can range from vicious to gentleman-like. The fiercer the competition, the more difficult the industry environment.

➤ New entry threats: The more difficult or substantial the barriers to entry, the more profitable the potential for the industry's players.

➤ Threat of substitute products or services: With numerous alternatives for the customers, the potential profitability declines. A monopolistic service, location, or product offering, the better the potential profitability.

➤ Bargaining power of suppliers: The more the suppliers can force increases in the costs of goods, and the less ability the company must pass on these increases (the fifth force), the stronger the squeezing effect on profitability.

➤ Bargaining power of buyers, or customers: The increasing ability of customers to find alternatives to shopping in your store, alternatives to services you provide, or alternate solutions, the stronger the pressure on profitability.

Porter's five forces and "conceptual tripod" can be combined in layman's terms, to understand how to offer a competitive global product locally:

➤ Know your customers: Without the base knowledge of your customers, and the ability to tailor your product to the individual markets, a product offering becomes generic and lacks differentiation.

➤ Understand the retail price sensitivity: Margin will only be maximized if you understand the retail flexibility of your product in each market. If a product is only treated as a commodity by the consumers, then profitability will be weakened.

➤ Watch for competitive products: Continuously keep an eye out for competitor uprisings. If your product can tackle a market, offer a solution to the consumer, and drive profitable sales, more than likely it will be copied very quickly by a competitor. As soon as a product is copied, the ability to price optimally decreases and the product becomes more of a commodity. This process is called "environmental scanning".

➤ Be entrepreneurial and passionate: Boring products are boring to consumers. A product should be marketed as light-hearted, solution-oriented, and ready to take on the world. Any other positioning leaves you vulnerable to competition.

The Boston Consulting Growth- Share Matrix is appropriate for understanding how to market each product inside its global operating environment:

➤ High annual real rate of market growth and high relative market share is labeled a "star". Everything is running smoothly in this quadrant, with product profitability growing, cash flow at neutral, and the strategy is to invest in growth.

➤ High annual real rate of market growth with low relative market share is labeled a "question mark." In this area, the product may be experiencing growth but so is the surrounding market; or, the growth may be just keeping up with the rest of the market. In this quadrant, the earnings are low, unstable, and growing, cash flow is negative, and the strategy is either to invest or divest. The products in this quadrant could become a money drain very quickly due to the competitive nature of the arena. The only way to compete and grow is through resource investment and profitability is going to be challenged.

➤ Low annual real rate of market growth with high relative market share is labeled a "cash cow". In this quadrant, earnings are high and stable, cash flow is positive, and the strategy is to "milk the cow." This strategy is not to be

confused with pacifism. In this quadrant, a product will vigorously defend its market share and fend off competitors.
- Low annual real rate of market growth with low relative market share is labeled a "dog." In this arena, earnings are low and unstable, cash flow is neutral or negative, and the strategy is to divest. Once in this quadrant, the best choice is to get out of the business and re-focus valuable resources elsewhere.

All the companies studied, whether a retailer or a consumer goods company, followed the four control levers described by Ross Simons. The four things that must happen effectively are as follows:
- Commitment is obtained as to the purpose of the company.
- Territory is effectively "staked out".
- The job is completed.
- The company is positioned for tomorrow.

The four control levers to use in setting a common operating guide throughout the company are as follows:
- Belief systems: Specific sets of beliefs that define basic values, purpose, and direction. The belief systems are in place to provide momentum and guidance to potential opportunities. These belief systems can be seen in mission statements, vision statements, credos, and statements of purpose.
- Boundary systems: Formally-stated rules and limits tied to defined sanctions and credible threat of punishment. The boundary systems are designed to allow personal creativity within defined limits of freedom. These boundary systems can be seen in codes of conduct, strategic planning systems, asset acquisition systems, and operational systems.
- Diagnostic control systems: Feedback systems that monitor organizational outcomes and correct deviations from preset standards of performance. These diagnostic control systems can be seen in profit plans and budgets, goals and objectives systems, project monitoring systems, and strategic planning systems.
- Interactive control systems: Systems that teams use to advance and develop. These control systems are used to focus the organization on strategic uncertainties, to provoke the emergence of new initiatives and strategies, to ensure the

way we do business relates very closely, and to address changes in customer needs.

Summary Findings:
- "One size fits all" cannot be used in a global setting. One would argue that this mantra cannot be used in any business setting. The brand essence of products and retail banners can remain the same. Local tastes, culture, and nuance drive the end-user connectivity needed to successfully compete.
- Customers are barraged with branding messages constantly throughout the day. Your message needs to be clear, concise, and able to connect where the customer wants to connect. Depending upon the demographic, the customers may want to connect by television, iPhone, radio, or sky messages. It does not matter what you, as the business, think will connect. It matters what you discover will connect with your customers by researching your customer base.
- Targeting high potential customer segments will enable the company to spend marketing dollars efficiently and effectively. Wasting marketing funds on customers who are not compelled to listen only dilutes the message.
- A brand-based culture is one that permeates every associate and every touch point of the company. The brand exists to give purpose and meaning to the existence of the company. One must work to establish a brand before crossing geographies.
- Understand customer product usage, not just demographic or nationality. End-usage is a much higher predictor of customer success than demographic or culture.
- Understanding your brand touch points will make the operating plan effective. From pre-purchase to purchase to post-purchase and influencing touch points, each step of customer connectivity needs a plan and execution.
- It is important not to confuse your definition of value with that of your customers. You need to know the business you are in (you do not sell televisions, you sell entertainment), understand your customer's highest need, and work to connect with your customers where they are talking.
- Environmental scanning is one of the most important aspects of global operating. Competitive moves, new entry threats,

substitute products, supplier power, and buyer power all play into the value offer of the retailer or consumer goods company.

- ➤ All products and markets should be allocated inside the Boston Consulting Growth- Share Matrix. By apportioning your products or services in this manner, you can manage your profitability, control expenses, direct resources where needed, and either divest or invest in the business.

Sample Retailer Review

Harvey's Wonderful Food Co-Op

Market Analysis
Strategies and Actions

Table of Contents

Market Analysis Purpose, Mission, Scope

<u>Purpose</u>
The purpose of this analysis is to analyze and synthesize the current market selling environment, while identifying key strengths- barriers to entry to be enhanced and protected, opportunities to be addressed, and external environmental threats to be reviewed for possible actions and tactical moves or alterations to the plan.

<u>Mission</u>
The mission of the analysis is to help Harvey's Wonderful Food Co-Op. The information is designed to assist in the further success and profitability of the co-op, and ongoing occupation of its unique niche in food retail.

<u>Scope</u>
The scope of the analysis is to analyze current competitors existing inside the Albany market, review all aspects of retail inside and out, and to also look at any key competitors that may have a plan to open in the market soon. Then, take those strengths, opportunities, and threats and aggregate them into clear and concise priorities, strategies, and actions.

Executive Summary

Harvey's Wonderful Food Co-Op (HWFC) is a retailer operating in the market that occupies a unique niche in food retail, primarily in the focus on strict product guidelines, natural and organic selection, bulk food offer, cheese and foodservice. Its members feel a sense of being part of a "club" that even the most venerable competitors do not experience.

With its unique place, HWFC has a focused and differentiated appeal to culinary experts, foodies, organic and natural casuals as well as extreme users, vegans, and all customers overtly practicing conscious capitalism in the sense of fair trade, sustainability, and environmental impact.

The following analysis will cover in detail how HWFC is currently benchmarking versus its competitors as well as how well it is reaching its own potential, competitors or not. The analysis is broken into three main areas: strengths- barriers to entry, opportunities, and threats. We do not cover weaknesses. We believe the word "weaknesses" implies an unwillingness on behalf of the retailer to act. It is our belief that any area that could be enhanced or improved is an opportunity. On the other end of the continuum, any strength or differentiator is a barrier to entry that sets HWFC apart from its competitors. The threats are uncontrollable external forces, which should be identified and reviewed on a quarterly basis.

The result of the analysis is that HWFC has the potential for an 8% to 10% sales increase if selective action areas are addressed and resources are applied to the areas!

Lastly, HWFC has a unique place in retail that serves as a value to its customers. With a focus on strengthening its position, and enacting a long-term plan for future power, HWFC will enjoy many more years of sales growth and ensuing profitability growth.

To summarize, Harvey's Wonderful Food Co-Op is perfectly situated to follow a trend in food consumption that shows no signs of leveling for quite some time. HWFC is a gem that, with the following steps added to the general strategic plan being developed, is poised for excellence. Greatness can be realized within HWFC's own four walls!

Current Environment

Harvey's Wonderful Food Co-Op (HWFC) is perfectly-aligned with current and future food and lifestyle trends for the major generations:

- Baby Boomers: Born 1946-1964, Age 50-69, 32% of population
- Generation X: Born 1965-1980, Age 34-50, 27% of population
- Millennials (Gen Y): Born after 1980, Age 18-34, 27% of population
- Centennials (Gen Z): Born after 2000

Millennials will comprise the majority of the workforce by 2025

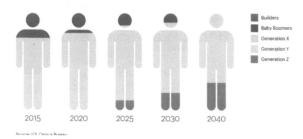

As Baby Boomers age and spending power diminishes, the next two generations will move to the forefront in societal impact. These generations have distinct impact on current and future retail trends. Overall consumer and retail trends are summarized in the following manner:

Formats are gone. The massive stores are too big. All formats are shrinking. Office stores sell food, mass merchants sell natural/organic, convenience stores sell breakfast, lunch, dinner. A contracted economy and evolving consumer has blurred all lines.

Accessibility of goods is seamless to the customer. Ordering online, buying in-store, pick-up, delivery, drones, ordering ahead, etc. are all part of the retailer relationship.
It is more about the experience than purchasing. Good food is sent out on Instagram, Facebook, and Twitter before being consumed. Referrals from friends, reviews on Yelp, and product recommendations from friends are more viable sources than advertisements or retailer-generated marketing. There are no borders between digital, social, in-store, or life for this generation.

Everyone cares about everything. Social, environmental, and health consciousness have moved to the forefront of purchase behavior. The Millennial generation is the first generation with a majority group that will move purchase decisions towards or away from retailers or products based upon social, environmental, or health consciousness. Included are fair trade, natural, organic, gluten free, sugar free, superberries, probiotics, waste impact, etc.

From the HWFC Mission Statement and Statements of Conscience below, there is a 100% overlap from HWFC to the Millennial generation, but not a 100% overlap from the Millennial generation to HWFC (especially in regards to format exclusivity and product accessibility). In addition, the shift from Utilitarian purchase-based in-store focus to experience-based in-store focus should be noted as a shift to be identified and fostered.

Harvey's Wonderful Food Co-Op

Mission Statement
Harvey's Wonderful is a member-owned and operated consumer cooperative that is committed to providing the community with affordable, high quality natural foods and products for healthy living. Our mission is to promote more equitable, participatory and ecologically sustainable ways of living. We welcome all who choose to participate in a community, which embraces cooperative principles, shares resources, and creates economic fairness in an atmosphere of cooperation and respect for humanity and the earth.

Statements of Conscience
- We are committed to our food policy, which reflects buying practices for food and body aids with consideration towards moral and ethical production, environmental stewardship, healthy living, and safety.
- We are committed to helping our community learn more about growing, choosing, preparing, and using natural foods.
- We are committed to learning and teaching about alternative ways of living that are healthy for ourselves, our community, and our planet.

- We are committed to encouraging an environment where ideas and philosophies can be generated, shared, and expressed freely.
- We support, embrace, and celebrate the diversity of our community.
- We are committed to providing our customers with knowledgeable staff and a positive shopping environment.
- We are committed to donating five percent (5%) of our net profits per year to local non-profit organizations.

The overlaps and the gaps between the generational trends and HWFC mission and vision identified above will be the focus of the market analysis.

Lifestyle of Health and Sustainability (LOHAS)

Now, we turn our attention to the growth of the chosen customer lifestyle track at HWFC: Lifestyle of Health and Sustainability (LOHAS). The LOHAS lifestyle is said to represent 19% of the adults in the United States and an estimated $290B in purchasing power.

LOHAS Tenets
Health
Environment
Social Justice
Personal Development
Sustainability

In each of the above tenets, HWFC has a clear representation, between natural and organic foods, nutritional products, integrated and homeopathic care (non-Rx), a robust event schedule, bulk foods, dietary supplements, and mind/ body/ spirit products. Clearly, the customer focus and alignment of HWFC was leading edge when formed in 1968. Many years of growth have been realized by the current strategy.

Among the trends from the last five years are the following, which will drive our product and assortment reviews of HWFC and its primary competitors.

Top Food Trends LOHAS Lifestyle
Produce as a differentiator
Food as fuel- protein and energy delivered wholesomely
Higher order benefits- bliss, relaxation yoga in a bottle
Leafy greens in every form- kale, watercress, spinach
Fortified waters
Chewy beverages- kombucha, live probiotics, greens
Mock meats- tofu, soybean, pea protein
Allergen free alternatives
Indulgence- nut butters, dark chocolates
South American/ African superfoods- acerola cherries, Macqui fruits, baobab
Bee-free honey
Green tea
Beets, peppers, quinoa, steel cut oatmeal
Wild versus farm-raised

Non-GMO

The trends listed in the above figure represent almost all food growth for the past five years. Projections for organic and natural food growth are seen to be over 12% CAGR for the next three years, then leveling at 8% growth for the five years following. Organic food is estimated to represent $105B in retail sales for 2015, up from $57B in 2010. Additionally, 38% of consumers purchasing organic foods just started this behavior in the last twelve months.

Today, though, the industry has shifted from HWFC being leading edge in representing the targeted lifestyle to HWFC's being impacted by a swath of new competition. Between the opening of Whole Foods, Trader Joe's, Healthy Living Market, and the massive proliferation of LOHAS lifestyle trend products in conventional stores, HWFC is at a juncture in its connection with core customers and its ability to recruit new members into the co-op family.

If HWFC is to represent current environmental trends, considering a large existing sales base plus the impact of new competition, comparable store sales trends of +5% should be expected for the next five years. The analysis and plan that follows should allow HWFC to realize growth of 8% to 10% for the next five years upon full implementation. An average sales volume of $545,000 per non-seasonally impacted week should be the goal.

Harvey's Wonderful Food Co-Op Strengths, Opportunities, Threats

Strengths- Barriers to Entry	
• Membership advocacy • Strict product standards • Trustability • "Club" atmosphere • Events • Culinary paradise • Apothecary- remedies	• Bulk program • Cheese program • Foodservice program • Local program • Organic variety • Craft/ local beer program
Opportunities	Threats
• Name recognition • Seasonal program • Produce • Bakery • Floral- freshness entrance • Deli/ Foodservice • Meat/ Seafood • Marketing- social, digital, in-store, external • Store brand • Loyalty program • Expansion • Pricing/ Dating integrity	• Evolving target customers • New entrants- format blurring, consolidation • Wegmans • Trends

The best news in the entire analysis is that Harvey's Wonderful Food Co-Op (HWFC) possesses numerous strengths/ barriers to entry that are completely controlled internally. The success of HWFC will be more heavily weighted on internal actions than external impacts. HWFC already has foot traffic, a higher purpose, a pleasant shopping experience, and strong barriers to entry. These strengths are differentiators that will set HWFC apart from competitors and are primary advocacy and loyalty areas. Barriers to entry are to be protected at all costs. The goal of all key strengths is to:
- Know what makes you special
- Understand impact on customers
- Enhance protective barriers

- Communicate strengths in all brand and marketing messages

As a point, strengths are pliable and evolutionary. For example, as customers continue to evolve and new generations enter the target market, HWFC will need to evolve ahead of and with the customer. The culinary connection will be an area to cultivate going forward as cooking at home is a trend that is only building in popularity.

HWFC Strengths- Barriers to Entry

The most valuable aspect of strengths is that they are internally controlled. A mindset that strengths are barriers to entry that in turn are cultivated throughout all facets of the business should be the goal. The strengths in the previous table can be divided into company-level and product-level.

Company-level Strengths
Membership advocacy: HWFC members pay a fee to join, plus receive a discount in exchange for work inside the store. In terms of connecting employees to direct company results, the co-op format offers an intrinsic link that most large chains only wish they could incorporate. Members and employees have a reason to care and a reason to shop in the store. Strong barrier to entry to be protected, enhanced and communicated in marketing messages.
"Protect the Barrier" action: Employee expertise for customer engagement. Does this format allow for the employee knowledge and engagement evident at Whole Foods?

Strict product standards: HWFC has a product standard manual as well as a membership that has input into all products. In a sense, the strict product standards allow a "piece of mind" to be had by all customers. The analysis has shown competitors operating in the natural/ organic space to be "blurring the lines" between steadfast adherence to product standards. Multiple examples where Whole Foods, Healthy Living and Trader Joe's have a wider collection of reasons an item can be carried (Free Trade, cage-free, non-GMO, local eggs, etc.). The strict product standards at HWFC should be communicated throughout the store and in all external marketing. One discussion point should be whether the strict guidelines or member input are limiting trend identification or sales volume opportunities (rotisserie chicken, bakery items, hams for Easter, lower price point milk, etc.).

"Protect the Barrier" action: As alternate formats add HWFC-type products to a general assortment, what is the consumer trade-off between exclusive HWFC experience and "complete the shop" convenience and affordability of the other formats?

Trustability: Because of the standards mentioned previously, the customers can trust HWFC has done their homework, understands the assortment needed for the target customer, and will ensure proper Quality Assurance is present in all levels of the business. HWFC must proactively develop and maintain an atmosphere that will allow the continuation of a trusting environment.

"Club" atmosphere: When interacting with HWFC shoppers, the store is a pleasurable shopping experience where you make plans to meet your friends, feel like you are part of the "club", and truly enjoy interacting with those around you. This level of in-store experience is only enjoyed by select few merchants in food retail. "Come in, browse the offer, meet your friends, have lunch, leave feeling good about your choices" should be cultivated as a reason to join and a reason to shop HWFC.

"Protect the Barrier" action: The lifeblood of the organization is going to be how well HWFC can acquire and integrate new members and the next generation of shoppers.

Events: The event calendar allows for the extension of the HWFC brand and lifestyle. HWFC's ability to fully align the event schedule with the target customer will be paramount. Fully define the various levels of target customers and integrate lifestyle even further into the event calendar and this strength will continue to bring value.

Culinary paradise: When shopping HWFC, there is a distinct feel as a "foodies paradise" that can be cultivated and enhanced. From cooking classes to live demos to cooking utensils to groupings by recipes and ingredients, all the makings are there to allow HWFC to be a leader in all things foodie.

"Protect the Barrier" action: The connection to healthy cooking and all available ingredients and cooking ideas is somewhat under-stated at HWFC.

Product-level Strengths

Apothecary- remedies: HWFC owns one of the most extensive selections of whole health body care and apothecary products in the area. Rivaled only by Whole Foods. Shout it in all media platforms. Clearly could be a destination trip for the engaged users.

"Protect the Barrier" action: HWFC does not operate a pharmacy, like Hannaford. Having an Rx in-house "completes the connection" between self-solutions and Rx solutions.

Bulk Program: One of the top selections of bulk foods in the market. A growing trend in food, representing culinary interests, packaging concerns, healthy alternatives, etc. Bulk Foods should be the destination for all consumers.

"Protect the Barrier" action: Bulk foods are relatively under-marketed at HWFC. Why use bulk foods, how to understand categorization, representation of certain categories, etc. should be addressed.

Cheese program: A top selection in the market, with heavily engaged employees. The cheese team members offer their favorites, make a point to interact with shoppers, have product knowledge, and know their varieties. Excellent department.

"Protect the Barrier" action: Is enough being done to help in passive selling of products? Signage depicting taste, bitterness versus smooth, creamy versus non-creamy, etc. is superior at Whole Foods and Wegmans.

Foodservice program: A major source of repeat and everyday traffic at HWFC. During heavy traffic times, the seating area is over-capacity. The hot bar especially is a local destination.

"Protect the Barrier" action: Whereas immediate consumption is being addressed, is enough being done for "take home" consumption? Organic rotisserie chickens, meal deals, ready to eat packs, etc. are secondary to immediate consumption but may offer a larger return if addressed. Whole Foods offers at least ten times the linear footage as HWFC, plus offers Indian, Chinese, pizza, etc.

Local program: Well represented in-store. Relationships with local farmers, dairy operators, center store purveyors, etc. is evident throughout the store.

"Protect the Barrier" action: Other competitors are catching up. All major supermarkets, plus Whole Foods and Trader Joes, offer some version of a local program. Find a way to differentiate HWFC's version of local.

Organic variety: One of the best representations in the marketplace. Truly, HWFC is a destination for organic variety. Ensure variety makes its way over to all departments, including meat, baked goods, deli, etc. Tout organic variety in all platforms.

"Protect the Barrier" action: Others are catching up. In addition to Whole Foods and Trader Joes, conventional grocery is on top of their game, especially Hannaford. One angle may be the fact that even Whole Foods "skirts the rules" at times to offer items that may or may not fit the strict product guidelines. At Whole Foods, being Fair Trade is good enough to carry an item. Healthy Living Market carries Tropicana Orange Juice and regular milk. HWFC may be the only ones left with strict all-encompassing product standards.

Craft/ Local Beer: Excellent variety and coverage of craft and local beers, including gluten free options and singles. Key product offering for the target demographic.

"Protect the Barrier" actions: Once again, the variety is matched by other traditional and non-traditional formats, including an almost identical variety at The Fresh Market and a "regular" variety on top of the craft/ local at Hannaford, Shop Rite, and Price Chopper. In addition, Price Chopper offers Growler Stations at select locales and most competitors offer a "Pick Six" mix and match section. Both are not offered at HWFC.

HWFC "Protect the Barrier" Action Checklist
- o Employee expertise for customer engagement.
- o Consumer trade-off between exclusive HWFC experience and "complete the shop" convenience and affordability of the other formats.
- o Acquire and integrate new members and the next generation of shoppers.
- o Make the connection to healthy cooking and all available ingredients and cooking ideas at HWFC.
- o Having an Rx in-house "completes the connection" between self-solutions and Rx solutions.
- o Marketing why use bulk foods, how to understand categorization, representation of certain categories, etc. should be addressed.

108

- Passive selling of cheese. Signage depicting taste, bitterness versus smooth, creamy versus non-creamy, etc. is superior at Whole Foods and Wegmans.
- Organic rotisserie chickens, meal deals, ready to eat packs, etc. are secondary to immediate consumption but may offer a larger return if addressed. Whole Foods offers at least ten times the linear footage as HWFC, plus offers Indian, Chinese, pizza, etc.
- Find a way to differentiate HWFC's version of local.
- HWFC may be the only ones left with strict all-encompassing product standards.
- Beer has an almost identical variety at The Fresh Market and a "regular" variety on top of the craft/ local at Hannaford, Shop Rite, and Price Chopper. In addition, Price Chopper offers Growler Stations at select locales and most competitors offer a "Pick Six" mix and match section. Both are not offered at HWFC.

HWFC Opportunities

Strengths- Barriers to Entry	
• Membership advocacy • Strict product standards • Trustability • "Club" atmosphere • Events • Culinary paradise • Apothecary- remedies	• Bulk program • Cheese program • Foodservice program • Local program • Organic variety • Craft/ local beer program
Opportunities	Threats
• Name recognition • Seasonal program • Produce • Bakery • Floral- freshness entrance • Deli/ Foodservice • Meat/ Seafood • Marketing- social, digital, in-store, external • Store brand • Loyalty program • Expansion • Pricing/ dating integrity	• Evolving target customers • New entrants- format blurring, consolidation • Wegmans • Trends

Opportunities are not weaknesses unless they are not identified nor pursued. All opportunities following are derived from competitor store visits, alternate market visits, category comparisons, and industry trends. With "Opportunities", they are ranked in order of relative scope and impact on HWFC's brand promise.

Name recognition: An informal local polling shows a clear difference between members and non-members in the actual understanding of what is offered by Harvey's Wonderful Food Co-Op. Members clearly understand the offer as natural, organic, and "good for you". Non-members had responses such as:
   o "I have no idea what they sell there."
   o "Isn't that a Weight Watchers store?"
   o "I'm not a member, so I am not allowed in that store."

o "I am not on a weight loss program, so why should I shop there?"

Most the non-member responses revolved around the word "Wonderful" in the name. There was no connection made in any of those surveyed between "Harvey's Wonderful" and bulk foods. No connection. The stores that were easily connected? Whole Foods, Healthy Living Market, Trader Joes, The Fresh Market, Walmart, and Shop Rite. Learned connections (not intuitive)? Hannaford, Price Chopper, Wegmans.

Action Suggestions:
⇒ Start an internal group to begin the discussion of name recognition.
⇒ Determine a direction for the company. Either build and strengthen the connection, change the name, or form a tagline making the connection.
❖ High priority, especially in terms of attracting new members.
❖ Potential sales benefit: TBD

Seasonal program: The major flow of newness in food stores is based upon the consistent in-flow and out-flow of seasonal programs. The objective of seasonal programs is to be ahead of the customer before the next season hits. Being ahead reminds the customers that "this is the place to go" when the season does finally hit. Or, it prompts an urge to buy on the spot. Holiday candy, for example, will be purchased three or four times before the actual holiday hits.

In multiple visits one and two weeks before Easter, there was very little representation of Easter items, such as extra egg displays, coloring kits, Easter lilies, Easter baskets, hams, cooking trays, etc. Produce was leading with apples and cider- fall items. Easter is a major food holiday and the store needed to reflect the upcoming holiday. On top, Easter usually signifies Spring, which means cooking outside, kebabs, etc.

Action Suggestions:
⇒ Immediate formation of seasonal program, including all departments.
⇒ Map out the calendar year.
⇒ Identify key holidays and seasons.
⇒ Align product and ad in-store merchandising.

⇒ Plan for entire store makeovers as seasons and holidays approach.

⇒ Integrate all marketing media platforms, including in-store signage, social and digital.

❖ High priority, especially in consideration of incremental sales and competitive edge.

❖ Potential sales benefit: Determined by implementation energy and timeline, but could range upwards of 4% overall sales increase. Based upon current average selling volume, a seasonal program could conservatively bring an incremental $20K per week ($1M incremental sales annually).

Produce: The produce offer is a key destination spot for most food shoppers, and is one of the highest-ranking considerations amongst HWFC's target market. In fact, some studies suggest produce as the top consideration of where to shop for 75% of consumers (followed by meat department and store brands). With a direct impact consideration for HWFC's target customer, this department should receive a high resource and expertise focus.

Action Suggestions:

⇒ Stadium impact in produce: start low and angle viewpoint higher as you move to the back of produce.

⇒ Sign kit with legible signs: extremely difficult signage to read, plus missing "passive selling" opportunities describing local, taste, recipes, etc.

⇒ Local message: As compared to Whole Foods, the local message is under-stated.

⇒ Baskets for sale over produce: Are they for sale, are they not? Prices? Tie-in?

⇒ Cider in March: entire seasonal make-over should happen as fruits and vegetables switch origins or seasons change.

⇒ Massive presence: very difficult to understand the sale items, "big deal" items, focus items, etc.

⇒ Green wall: should be used as a differentiator. Angle it properly, keep it fresh, communicate uses of greens. Whole Foods and Price Chopper have excellent benchmarks. Healthy Living Market does not have a green wall.

⇒ Trends: Increase visibility of latest trends- superberries, watercress, kale, spinach, red grapes, etc.

⇒ Asian presence- HWFC is in the center of a high Asian customer base, but has very little representation of Asian foods.

⇒ Peppers assortment: one of the hottest trends in food is pepper variety. Done best at Whole Foods, Wegmans, and Price Chopper.

⇒ Inconsistent produce: even on items sold by the "each", the quality is inconsistent (pineapple example).

⇒ Describe hydroponic expand in-store: excellent trend. Mention what is carried and play it up in multi-media platforms.

⇒ Massive apples as Easter approaches: Seasonality is an issue that needs to be immediately addressed.

⇒ Under assorted produce beverages: Bolthouse, Pom, Acai, Aloe, etc. Almost every fruit and vegetable is offered in a liquid form.

⇒ Tons of cider: seasonal issue for March.

⇒ Cut fruit variety: whether cut in-store or purchased cut, this section should be prominent. Whole Foods, Wegmans, Price Chopper, Shop Rite all have strong cut fruit sections. Whole Foods also has 16 linear feet of cut vegetables.

⇒ Stages of bananas: quality assurance in banana purchasing is essential. Plus, Wegmans and Whole Foods are heavy tonnage organic banana sellers, Healthy Living adds Fair Trade designation.

⇒ Organization in produce: need a planogram or flowgram. Peppers in multiple locations, tomatoes in multiple locations, etc.

⇒ Store footprint: produce may be under-sized based upon the potential of the department. If hard-wired refrigeration prevents expansion, consider auxiliary displays throughout the store.

❖ High priority considering target customer overlap.

❖ Potential sales benefit: Based upon the under-statement of meat at HWFC and the increased focus of produce by target customers, we should expect produce to have a run rate of 22% to 25% of weekly sales. Current average is 15% to 17%. Hitting expected run rate would make produce a $6.8M category for HWFC, an increase of roughly $40K per week on average store base of $505K per week. If netting 30% post-shrink profit rates, HWFC could realize an incremental annual $2M in sales and $600K net profit.

Bakery: Product considerations need to be made in the bakery. Given the dietary and nutritional guidelines, the department will require a high competency level. But, the resource allocation should show an acceptable rate of return. Natural, organic, gluten free, sprouted, etc. considerations can be found either in a thaw n serve form or baked in-store; and are available for all sub-categories (artisan bread, French bread, desserts, bagels, doughnuts, tortillas, cookies, etc.
Action Suggestions:
> Form a study immediately to identify those products available to sell under strict HWFC guidelines.
> Map a commodity plan for each sub-category of the bakery (artisan bread, French bread, desserts, bagels, doughnuts, tortillas, cookies, etc.).
> Establish buying plan and implementation timeline.
> Determine location to present a bountiful appearance in-store. One suggestion could be in front of the cheese section.
❖ High priority, based upon almost non-existent variety today.
❖ Potential sales benefit: HWFC should expect bakery to reach 3% of sales, or $787K annually. At a net gross profit of 50% post-shrink, HWFC should realize $394K net gross profit.

Floral- freshness entrance: Floral departments are freshness image setters. When located at the front of the store and merchandised for impulse purchases, floral departments set the fresh tone for the rest of the store. On average, HWFC should expect sales of $8,000 per week at a net margin of 50%. On holidays, especially Valentine's Day and Easter, the sales number could reach 10% of sales for the week, when merchandised properly.
Action Suggestions:
> Form an annual plan for floral, considering seasonality and assortment to match the season (poinsettias, Easter lilies, Roses, bedding plants, etc. all have seasonal hits that will bring the department to life.
> The front entrance and vestibule should only be floral and produce products that scream freshness and seasonal excitement!

- ⇒ Move the bulletin board to the hallway towards the restroom, move the seed packets, little shopping carts, anything that is not floral and produce.
- ❖ High priority, based upon the HWFC image and brand promise.
- ❖ Potential sales benefit: HWFC should expect floral sales to be double current run rates. Freshness entrance impact halo effect cannot be measured.

Deli/ Foodservice: Encompassing food consumed on-site as well as food prepared for in-home use, the deli/ foodservice area provides the greatest opportunity for repeat and multiple visits. Understanding the role of deli/ foodservice, a plan will need to be developed to address trends, newness, product tonnage, etc. The plan should be developed separating deli, breakfast, lunch, dinner, hot, cold, in-store consumed, and take-home.

Action Suggestions:
- ⇒ "Food type" plan to be developed for breakfast, lunch, and dinner.
- ⇒ Food offers to be addressed and discussed for potential to be carried at HWFC. For example, rotisserie chickens are the number one tonnage item in many competitor foodservice areas. HWFC does not carry rotisserie chickens. Whole Foods and Wegmans carry organic rotisserie chickens for $13.99.
- ⇒ Identify full missing categories carried at competitors, such as sushi. Wegmans carries a full line of quinoa brown rice sushi. Pizza is stronger at Price Chopper and Whole Foods, while not carried at Hannaford or The Fresh Market. Wegmans has one of the most competitive sub programs in the industry.
- ⇒ The "power aisle" with the hot bar as the center focus could be used more optimally for increased immediate consumption items, like Healthy Living, Fresh Market, Whole Foods, Shop Rite, and Wegmans.
- ⇒ Beer is not for immediate consumption in-store, and could be moved to the back section by the cheese. The subsequent space could be used for to-go packs, increased beverages, snacks, meals to go.

⇒ Consider the value of placing a checkout in the foodservice area to be operated during peak hours and take pressure off the front-end.

⇒ Make a deli plan by lunch meats and deli salads. All major competitors have an organic selection available in the deli, with Wegmans doing the best job showcasing their offer.

⇒ Consider some type of "repeat purchase" loyalty program for continuous patrons of the foodservice area.

❖ High priority, based upon missing high tonnage categories.

❖ Potential sales benefit: TBD by commodities added (rotisserie chickens could be 10% of total foodservice sales, sushi is a target market match and is not offered at HWFC, pizza can be offered as a full program with commitment, etc.)

Meat/ Seafood: Understanding current restrictions at HWFC, it must still be stated that the majority of competitors average 22% of total store sales in meat and 4% of total store sales in seafood. At an HWFC average of 7% of total store sales, the meat and seafood departments have tremendous upside potential. If the % rate were to double, it would mean an average extra $35K per week, or $1.8M in sales annually. At 14%, HWFC would still be considerably under the regular shopping rate of customers.

Action Suggestions:

⇒ Consider the limitations as well as the upside potential and address the gaps.

⇒ Consider the "complete the shop" aspect of carrying a large portion of the plate that has not been covered previously.

❖ High priority, based upon competitor %'s as rate to sales.

❖ Potential sales benefit: Could realize between $2M to $4M incremental annual sales.

Marketing: HWFC has a great story to tell! Wholesome food, co-op, organic, bulk foods, sustainability, Fair Trade, etc. Between telling the HWFC story internally and externally, a cohesive message carrying the brand throughout all customer touchpoints is extremely important. Why shop here? What are the differentiators? How can we connect? What do we stand for? What kind of food do we carry? Why are we different? Every platform, every message, every connection with the customer should carry the same underlying message.

Action Suggestions:

⇒ Form a comprehensive plan describing the basic under-lying message, plus the seasonally-relevant marketing message that will be present in all aspects of customer connectivity.

⇒ Include in-store communication, external communication, social, digital, print, mobile, audio. All platforms have a role in communicating the message.

⇒ Social media: HWFC's Instagram account is well aligned with the core message. Facebook and Twitter mostly are only posting menu items with no pictures. Should be aligned.

⇒ In-store: Devoid of messages around social purpose, locations of sections, culinary or earth décor, etc.

⇒ The road communication is under-stated and confusing. What looks like the back of the store is the main area for parking. No road sign compounds the issue.

→ Is the CDTA bus program reaching your target customer?

❖ High priority, mainly due to impact on current and future customer connectivity.

❖ Potential sales benefit: TBD, but a lack of marketing claiming your space allows other competitors to take that space.

Store brand: All competitors possess some type of three-tier store brand program (opening price point, national brand equivalent, and value-added tier). HWFC has a limited assortment, primarily in the vitamin and supplement section. The benefits of a store brand program include repeat purchases, store loyalty, in-house advertising, value message, and margin enhancement.

Action Suggestions:

⇒ Form a plan for a store brand procurement source, whether a consolidator or a wholesaler. More than likely, the volume minimums will not be attainable by HWFC alone.

⇒ Decide the tiers needed and number of sku's possible.

⇒ Form timeline and implementation plan.

❖ Medium priority, based upon benefit enhancement. Effort will be high.

❖ Potential sales benefit: TBD, determined by number of sku's, departments, sourcing, etc. Most retailers aim for a 25% store brand penetration with an average of 10% higher margin rate. Could mean $650,000 incremental net margin, not counting qualitative benefits.

Loyalty program: The future of retailing lies in the use of big data to personalize the customer engagement. The retailer trades a customer discount in exchange for the customer's data. The data is then used to enhance the relationship as well as efficiently and effectively the marketing funds. Except for Fresh Market, Whole Foods, and Healthy Living, all competitors have a loyalty card.

Action Suggestions:
⇒ Decide if HWFC has the resources and desire to pursue the opportunity.
⇒ If yes, develop the plan.
❖ Medium priority, as some data collection can happen "generically" as opposed to customer-specific, and can still be used to promote complementary items.
❖ Potential sales benefit: TBD

Expansion: Inevitably, aggregated volume would be a stronger future position for HWFC than a sole unit. But, expansion would be its own plan, to include target market, real estate direction, best fit, acquire or build ground-up, continued synergies of fixed costs (including advertising and media), etc.

Action Suggestions:
⇒ Decide upon necessity of expansion.
⇒ Determine financial impact and viability.
⇒ In the market, it has been heard that Healthy Living in Saratoga is for sale. Recommendation is not to buy, based upon mall location. Investigation in-store and externally reveals a strong disappointment by Healthy Living in their current results, which is forcing them to go into "shrink control" mode as well as diluting their brand (carrying mainstream items just for tonnage).
⇒ Between Clifton Park and Saratoga would be the most natural target market match for HWFC.
⇒ We do not know of any Wegmans plans at this time, but they are probably the most secretive of any retailer for Albany plans.
⇒ Whole Foods, Fresh Market, and Trader Joe's could easily open at least one more store in the Saratoga area.
⇒ Price Chopper is re-branding to Market 32, which includes a heavier collection of natural and organic, as well it will build customer buzz and interest.

⇒ Shop Rite is satisfied with half their results (Niskayuna and Central Avenue) and would like to see improved results at their other two stores (Colonie and Slingerlands).

⇒ Hannaford is only remodeling in Albany, with no public plans for new sites.

⇒ One competitor to watch, and it is a perfect overlap for customers, is Adams out of the Downstate area. Showing double digit growth in their three stores, and Albany would be a natural expansion area.

⇒ No expansion plans into Albany for Ahold.

⇒ Kroger is a continuous rumor for northeast expansion, although it is not known if Albany area would be first (unless they acquire).

Pricing/ dating integrity: Multiple examples of line families of brands with varying retail prices, as well out of date items on the shelf and product rotation needs. These two issues are the basics of running the operation, have multiple margin and customer confidence impacts, and could lead to health issues if out of date product is sold.

Action Suggestions:

⇒ Immediate implementation and training of product rotation plan, focusing on key areas first (dairy).

⇒ Review and implementation of pricing program, to link like sku's, ensure price changes are completed in a timely manner and reflect all cost increases through retail changes immediately, for margin enhancement or control.

HWFC Opportunities Action Checklist

o Start an internal group to begin the discussion of name recognition.

o Determine a direction for the company. Either build and strengthen the connection, change the name, or form a tagline making the connection.

o Immediate formation of seasonal program, including all departments.

o Map out the calendar year.

o Identify key holidays and seasons.

o Align product and ad in-store merchandising.

o Plan for entire store makeovers as seasons and holidays approach.

- Integrate all marketing media platforms, including in-store signage, social and digital.
- Stadium impact in produce: start low and angle viewpoint higher as you move to the back of produce.
- Sign kit with legible signs: extremely difficult signage to read, plus missing "passive selling" opportunities describing local, taste, recipes, etc.
- Local message: As compared to Whole Foods, the local message is under-stated.
- Baskets for sale over produce: Are they for sale, are they not? Prices? Tie-in?
- Cider in March: entire seasonal make-over should happen as fruits and vegetables switch origins or seasons change.
- Massive presence: very difficult to understand the sale items, "big deal" items, focus items, etc.
- Green wall: should be used as a differentiator. Angle it properly, keep it fresh, communicate uses of greens. Whole Foods and Price Chopper have excellent benchmarks. Healthy Living Market does not have a green wall.
- Trends: Increase visibility of latest trends- superberries, watercress, kale, spinach, red grapes, etc.
- Asian presence- HWFC is in the center of a high Asian customer base, but has very little representation of Asian foods.
- Peppers assortment: one of the hottest trends in food is pepper variety. Done best at Whole Foods, Wegmans, and Price Chopper.
- Inconsistent produce: even on items sold by the "each", the quality is inconsistent (pineapple example).
- Describe hydroponic expand in-store: excellent trend. Mention what is carried and play it up in multi-media platforms.
- Massive apples as Easter approaches: Seasonality is an issue that needs to be immediately addressed.
- Under assorted produce beverages: Bolthouse, Pom, Acai, Aloe, etc. Almost every fruit and vegetable is offered in a liquid form.
- Tons of cider: seasonal issue for March.
- Cut fruit variety: whether cut in-store or purchased cut, this section should be prominent. Whole Foods, Wegmans, Price

Chopper, Shop Rite all have strong cut fruit sections. Whole Foods also has 16 linear feet of cut vegetables.

- Stages of bananas: quality assurance in banana purchasing is essential. Plus, Wegmans and Whole Foods are heavy tonnage organic banana sellers, Healthy Living adds Fair Trade designation.
- Organization in produce: need a planogram or flowgram. Peppers in multiple locations, tomatoes in multiple locations, etc.
- Store footprint: produce may be under-sized based upon the potential of the department. If hard-wired refrigeration prevents expansion, consider auxiliary displays throughout the store.
- Form a study immediately to identify those products available to sell under strict HWFC guidelines.
- Map a commodity plan for each sub-category of the bakery (artisan bread, French bread, desserts, bagels, doughnuts, tortillas, cookies, etc.).
- Establish buying plan and implementation timeline.
- Determine location to present a bountiful appearance in-store. One suggestion could be in front of the cheese section.
- Form an annual plan for floral, considering seasonality and assortment to match the season (poinsettias, Easter lilies, Roses, bedding plants, etc. all have seasonal hits that will bring the department to life.
- The front entrance and vestibule should only be floral and produce products that scream freshness and seasonal excitement!
- Move the bulletin board to the hallway towards the restroom, move the seed packets, little shopping carts, anything that is not floral and produce.
- "Food type" plan to be developed for breakfast, lunch, and dinner.
- Food offers to be addressed and discussed for potential to be carried at HWFC. For example, rotisserie chickens are the number one tonnage item in most competitor foodservice areas. HWFC does not carry rotisserie chickens. Whole Foods and Wegmans carry organic rotisserie chickens for $13.99.
- Identify full missing categories carried at competitors, such as sushi. Wegmans carries a full line of quinoa brown rice sushi.

Pizza is stronger at Price Chopper and Whole Foods, while not carried at Hannaford or The Fresh Market. Wegmans has one of the most competitive sub programs in the industry.

- The "power aisle" with the hot bar as the center focus could be used more optimally for increased immediate consumption items, like Healthy Living, Fresh Market, Whole Foods, Shop Rite, and Wegmans.
- Beer is not for immediate consumption in-store, and could be moved to the back section by the cheese. The subsequent space could be used for to-go packs, increased beverages, snacks, meals to go.
- Consider the value of placing a checkout in the foodservice area to be operated during peak hours and take pressure off the front-end.
- Make a deli plan by lunch meats and deli salads. All major competitors have an organic selection available in the deli, with Wegmans doing the best job showcasing their offer.
- Consider some type of "repeat purchase" loyalty program for continuous patrons of the foodservice area.
- Consider the limitations as well as the upside potential and address the gaps.
- Consider the "complete the shop" aspect of carrying a large portion of the plate that has not been covered previously.
- Form a comprehensive plan describing the basic under-lying message, plus the seasonally-relevant marketing message that will be present in all aspects of customer connectivity.
- Include in-store communication, external communication, social, digital, print, mobile, audio. All platforms have a role in communicating the message.
- Social media: HWFC's Instagram account is well aligned with the core message. Facebook and Twitter mostly are only posting menu items with no pictures. Should be aligned.
- In-store: Devoid of messages around social purpose, locations of sections, culinary or earth décor, etc.
- The road communication is under-stated and confusing. What looks like the back of the store is really the main area for parking. No road sign compounds the issue.
- Is the CDTA bus program reaching your target customer?
- Form a plan for a store brand procurement source, whether a consolidator or a wholesaler. More than likely, the volume minimums will not be attainable by HWFC alone.

- Decide the tiers needed and number of sku's possible.
- Form timeline and implementation plan.
- Decide if HWFC has the resources and desire to pursue the opportunity.
- If yes, develop the plan.
- Decide upon necessity of expansion.
- Determine financial impact and viability.
- In the market, it has been heard that Healthy Living in Saratoga is for sale. Recommendation is not to buy, based upon mall location. Investigation in-store and externally reveals a strong disappointment by Healthy Living in their current results, which is forcing them to go into "shrink control" mode as well as diluting their brand (carrying mainstream items just for tonnage).
- Between Clifton Park and Saratoga would be the most natural target market match for HWFC.
- We do not know of any Wegmans plans at this time, but they are probably the most secretive of any retailer for Albany plans.
- Whole Foods, Fresh Market, and Trader Joe's could easily open at least one more store in the Saratoga area.
- Price Chopper is re-branding to Market 32, which includes a heavier collection of natural and organic, as well it will build customer buzz and interest.
- Shop Rite is satisfied with half their results (Niskayuna and Central Avenue) and would like to see improved results at their other two stores (Colonie and Slingerlands).
- Hannaford is only remodeling in Albany, with no public plans for new sites.
- One competitor to watch, and it is a perfect overlap for customers, is Adams out of the Downstate area. Showing double digit growth in their three stores, and Albany would be a natural expansion area.
- No expansion plans into Albany for Ahold.
- Kroger is a continuous rumor for northeast expansion, although it is not known if Albany area would be first (unless they acquire).
- Immediate implementation and training of product rotation plan, focusing on key areas first (dairy).
- Review and implementation of pricing program, to link like sku's, ensure price changes are completed in a timely

manner and reflect all cost increases through retail changes immediately, for **margin** enhancement or control.

Strengths- Barriers to Entry	
• Membership advocacy • Strict product standards • Trustability • "Club" atmosphere • Events • Culinary Paradise • Apothecary- remedies	• Bulk program • Cheese program • Foodservice program • Local program • Organic variety • Craft/ local beer variety
Opportunities	Threats
• Name recognition • Seasonal program • Produce • Bakery • Floral- freshness entrance • Deli/ Foodservice • Meat/ Seafood • Marketing- social, digital, in-store, external • Store brand • Loyalty program • Expansion • Pricing/ dating integrity	• Evolving customers • New entrants- format blurring, consolidation • Wegmans • Trends

Threats to HWFC, in this study, can be defined as those external threats against which there is very little control. The best solution is to remain aware of the identified threats and place internal focus to ensure the threats are reviewed on a quarterly basis. You cannot alter the threat, but you can always position HWFC to accentuate barriers to entry and mitigate threat impacts.

Evolving customers: The natural and organic customer is evolving as the next generation gains more buying power. From being a "fringe" of the population, today's natural and organic customer is becoming more mainstream and more overall socially conscious. The data shows health and wellness will remain on its current strong trend for the undeterminable future. Added to that trend will be sustainability, social consciousness, a desire to spend less and less on everything,

125

and a desire to be socially and digitally connected to their retailers. There is a certain platform agnosticism that forces the need to discuss online ordering and delivery/ pick-up, in-store mobile deals, endless aisles online, extreme personalization, etc. Be assured, though, all parties must be onboard before embarking into online ordering for delivery or pick-up.

New entrants- format blurring, consolidation: With the growth in attractiveness for natural and organic products, all retailers are entering the market in some manner. From "pure play" retailers like Whole Foods to "complete shop" retailers like Hannaford, Shop Rite, and Price Chopper to "mass merchant" retailers like Walmart and Target, all formats are seeing the benefit of carrying more food and more natural and organic food as well. Pallets of Ella's Kitchen baby food are available at Walmart, along with over 120 Wild Oats organic items. Aldi has a complete branded gluten-free line. With this blurring of channels, HWFC will see the benefit of discussing how well it can maintain its rigid product guidelines while all other formats are adding item after item that was once only found at HWFC.

Wegmans: A Wegmans entry into the market would be a game changer for all area retailers. They are the number-one voted supermarket in the country year after year, have one of the widest selections of natural and organic of any competitors, and offer the customer the ability to complete the shop with extensive foodservice, competitive center store prices, club packs, and high customer engagement. On top, the other retailers' reactions to Wegmans would bring the competitive environment to a fever pitch.

Trends: As soon as superberries are the rage, along comes kale. As soon as kale is integrated into every form of food possible, along comes watercress, or ancient grains, or quinoa, or spinach, or detox, etc. Trends in food are happening at a lightning pace. HWFC will need to ensure there is a "watchdog" to identify and cover trends as they happen or even before they happen. HWFC's niche is only accentuated when a trend is identified and covered in HWFC first.

Conclusion

Harvey's Wonderful Food Co-Op is perfectly aligned with the trends and growth in food for now and into the future. As with all positive trends though, competitors are aiming to participate as well. The good news is that HWFC could see an 8% to 10% sales increase by enacting the above in-store actions! There is a tremendous amount of potential right at your fingertips. The above analysis and action points have been designed to format a strategy and plan around prioritized strengths and opportunities, along with a keen eye on uncontrollable threats.

HWFC will be strong even if none of the above items are acted upon. But, enacted and implemented....the sky is the limit!

14- Conclusion

This book has helped put together consumer trends, category management principles, store brand tactics, and a sample retailer analysis- all you need is passion! Add passion to fundamentals, and you're going to rock! Go for it!

Sources

Abreu Filho, Gilberto Duarte de; Calicchio, Nicola; Lunardini, Fernando. (2003). Brand Building in Emerging Markets. The McKinsey Quarterly. 2003 Special Edition: The Value in Organization. pp. 6-9.

Ackerman, Elise. (2008). eBay Tops Analysts' Estimates. McClatchy- Tribune Business News. Retrieved ProQuest: November 21, 2008. ProQuest document ID: 1464024231.

Acosta. (2018). The Why Behind the Buy.

Alon, Ilon. (2004). International Market Selection for a Small Enterprise: A Case Study in International Entrepreneurship. SAM Advanced Management Journal. 69(1).

Aisner, James. (2000). Global Brands: Connecting With Consumers Across Boundaries. Harvard Business School Working Knowledge. pp. 1-4. Retrieved May 16, 2008. http://hbswk.hbs.edu/item/1621.html.

Anheuser-Busch personal interview with Steve Burrows, CEO and President Anheuser-Busch Asia Inc. May 12, 2008.

Anonymous. (2004). Coca-Cola India in 2004- Marketing Strategy. ICM Center for Management. Retrieved: January 20, 2009. www.icmrindia.org.

Anonymous. (2008). Itochu Announces Investment in Major China Food Maker. Jiji Press English News Service. Retrieved ProQuest: November 21, 2008. ProQuest document ID: 1598796521.

Anonymous. (2008). Karina's Kolumn. The Banker. pp. 1-3. Retrieved ProQuest: May 16, 2008. ProQuest document ID: 1471488731.

Anonymous. (2005). P&G Groomed for Global Dominance: Gillette Strives for Cutting-Edge Expertise. Strategic Direction. 21(10). pp. 12-15. Retrieved ProQuest: May 16, 2008. ProQuest document ID: 928560381.

Anonymous. (2009). German Blames Coke for Diabetes. The Financial Express. Retrieved: January 20, 2009. www.financialexpress.com.

Anonymous. (2008). The Four Levers of Control. Career Development Plan. Retrieved: July 7, 2008. www.careerdevelopmentplan.net.

Anonymous. (2008). Yatinoo Announces International Expansion Strategy and Positions Itself in Contrast to Google, Yahoo, EBay, and Others. PR Newswire. Retrieved ProQuest: November 21, 2008. ProQuest document ID: 1581152811.

Anonymous Personal Interview. (2009). Interview with anonymous person serving as Chief Operating Officer of the un-disclosed company. August 4, 2009.

Antoncic, Bostjan; Hisrich, Robert. (2003). Privatization, Corporate Entrepreneurship, and Performance: Testing a Normative Model. Journal of Developmental Entrepreneurship. 8(3).

Apps, Peter. (2007). Backing Business in Africa. Alertnet. Retrieved: August 3, 2009. www.alertnet.org.

Argandona, Antonio. (2004). On Ethical, Social, and Environmental Management Systems. Journal of Business Ethics. 51(1).

Asda. (2007). Customer Services Asda: Frequently Asked Questions. Asda. November 1, 2007. Retrieved: June 8, 2009. www.wikipedia.org.

Attwood, James. (2009). Wal-Mart Completes Takeover of Chilean Grocer D&S. Bloomberg. www.bloomberg.com. January 23, 2009. Retrieved: June 8, 2009. www.wikipedia.org.

Auto News. (2007). Global Brands Suffer Power Drain According to GFK Roper Consulting Annual Worldwide....Auto News. pg. 1. Retrieved May 16, 2008. http://www.automotive.com/auto-news/02/30592/index.html.

Balfour, Frederick. (2006). TOM Online: eBay's Last China Card. Business Week (Online). Retrieved ProQuest: November 21, 2008. ProQuest document ID: 1183368161.

Ball, Deborah. (2007). After Buying Binge, Nestle Goes on a Diet; Departing CEO Slashes Slow Sellers, Brands; "No" to Low-Carb Rolo. Wall Street Journal. pp. 1-5. Retrieved ProQuest: May 16, 2008. http://proquest.umi.com.

Balwani, Samir. (2009). 5 Easy Social Media Wins for your Small Business. Mashable.com. Retrieved: August 21, 2009. www.mashable.com.

Barbaro, Michael. (2007). It's Not Only About Price At Wal-Mart. New York Times. March 2, 2007. Retrieved: June 8, 2009. www.wikiepdia.org.

Barrett, Hilton; Balloun, Joseph; Weinstein, Art. (2000). Marketing Mix Factors as Moderators of the Corporate Entrepreneurship- Business Performance Relationship- A Multistage, Multivariate Analysis. Journal of Marketing Theory and Practice.

Bartlett, Christopher; Goshal, Sumantra. (1996). Release the Entrepreneurial Hostages from your Corporate Hierarchy. Strategy & Leadership. 24(4).

BBC News. (2006). Nestle Takes the World Ice Cream Lead. Retrieved: June 8, 2009. www.wikipedia.org.

BBC News. (2003). Tesco Buys Japanese Retailer. BBC News. Retrieved: June 8, 2009. www.wikipedia.org.

Beckett, Robert. (2003). Communication Ethics: Principle and Practice. Journal of Communications Management. 8(1).

Berner, Robert. (2005). Can Wal-Mart Wear a White Hat? Business Week. September 22, 2005. Retrieved: June 8, 2009. www.wikipedia.org.

Birkinshaw, Julian. (1997). Entrepreneurship in Multinational Corporations: The Characteristics of Subsidiary Initiatives. Strategic Management Journal. 18(3).

Black, Leeora; Hartel, Charmine. (2003). The Five Capabilities of Socially Responsible Companies. Journal of Public Affairs. 4(2).

Bloom, Matt. (2004). The Ethics of Compensation Systems. Journal of Business Ethics. 52(2).

Brinkmann, Johannes. (2004). Looking at Consumer Behavior in a Moral Perspective. Journal of Business Ethics. 51(2).

Brand Strategy. (2007). Branding in China: Building a Successful Relationship with China. Brand Strategy. Retrieved ProQuest: November 26, 2008. ProQuest document ID: 1286598111.

Bryant, Adam. (2009). In a Word, He Wants Simplicity. NRF Smartbrief. Retrieved: July 23, 2009. www.nrf.com.

Buckley, Neil. (1995). People: Leahy Rings Tesco's Tills. Financial Times. pg. 40. Retrieved: June 8, 2009. www.wikipedia.org.

Bulik, Beth Snyder. (2008, March). THIS BRAND MAKES YOU MORE CREATIVE. Advertising Age, 79(12), 4,27. Retrieved April 24, 2008, from ABI/INFORM Global database. (Document ID: 1452547301).

Bush, Michael. (2008, April 14). Coffee Klatsch 2.0. Marketing Magazine, pg 14.

Business Insider. (2013). Top 20 Trends. http://www.businessinsider.com/business-insider-us-20-2013-2013-11?op=1#ixzz2IKQiChaf

Business Network. (2008). Retrieved: June 8, 2009. www.wikipedia.org.

Business Pundit. (2009). 10 Essential Twitter Tools for Business. Business Pundit. April 8, 2009. Retrieved: August 24, 2009. www.businesspundit.com.

Business Week. (2001). Viral Marketing Alert! Business Week. www.businessweek.com. Retrieved: June 8, 2009. www.wikipedia.org.

Business Week. (2005). Wal-Mart's British Accent Needs Polish. Business Week. Retrieved: November 26, 2008. http://www.businessweek.com/magazine/content/05_47/b3960070.html.

Caltrout. (2009). www.caltrout.org article. Retrieved: June 8, 2009. www.wikipedia.org.

Capio, Ralph J.; Capio, Christopher. (1998). The United States- Cuba Relationship: A Time for a Change? Air and Space Power Journal- Chronicles Online Journal. Retrieved: July 23, 2009. www.airpower.maxwell.af.mil.

Carrefour. (2009). Annual Results 2008. Carrefour Group. www.carrefour.com. Retrieved: June 8, 2009. www.wikipedia.org.

Cascio, Tim. (2009). Mobile Marketing: 50 Ways to Promote Your iPhone App. Mobile Marketing, Monetization, and Methods. June 18, 2009. Retrieved: August 24, 2009. www.timcascio.wordpress.com.

Chatterjee, Anjan; Jauchius, Matthew; Kaas, Hans-Werner; Satpathy, Aurobind. (2002). Revving up auto branding. The McKinsey Quarterly. 1. pp. 134-143.

Chen, Jin; Zhang, Cheng; Yuan, YuFei; Huang, Lihua. (2007). Understanding the Emerging C2C Electronic Market in China. Electronic Markets. 17(2). Retrieved ProQuest: November 21, 2008. ProQuest document ID: 1271721871.

Child, Peter; Heywood, Suzanne; Kliger, Michael. (2002). Do Retail Brands Travel? The McKinsey Quarterly. 1. pp. 11-13.

China Daily. (2004). Nestle Urged to Tell Truth About GMO's. Retrieved: June 8, 2009. www.wikipedia.org.

China Milk Scandal Claims Victim Outside Mainland. (2008). Retrieved: June 8, 2009. www.wikipedia.org.

Class PowerPoint. (2008). Dynamic Strategic Management. Boston Consulting Growth-Share Matrix. pg. 22.

Colchester, Max. (2007). Nescafe Brews Buzz via Blogs; Marketers are Enlisting Online Communities to Help Craft Pitches. Wall Street Journal. pp. 1-3. Retrieved ProQuest: May 16, 2008. ProQuest document ID: 1387169791.

Cordeiro, William. (2003). The Only Solution to the Decline in Business Ethics: Ethical Managers. Teaching Business Ethics. 7(3).

Corkran, Michael. (2008). Taming the Market Lion of Tomorrow. Mergers and Acquisitions. 43(11). Retrieved ProQuest: November 21, 2008. ProQuest document ID: 1598872141.

Corporate Watch. (2007). Unilever Environmental Pollution. Corporate Watch. www.corporatewatch.org.uk. Retrieved: June 8, 2009. www.wikipedia.org.
Court, David; French, Thomas; McGuire, Tim; Partington, Michael. Marketing in 3-D. The McKinsey Quarterly. 4. pp. 6-17.
Court, David; Leiter, Mark; Loch, Mark. (1999). Brand Leverage. The McKinsey Quarterly (2) 101.

Cuban Economy. (1998). Cuban Economy. Tulane. Retrieved: July 23, 2009. www.tulane.edu.

Cui, Geng; Choudhury, Pravat. (2003). Consumer Interests and the Ethical Implications of Marketing. The Journal of Consumer Affairs. 37(2).

Custom Web Express. www.customwebexpress.com. Retrieved: June 8, 2009. www.wikipedia.org.

Daboub, Anthony; Calton, Jerry. (2002). Stakeholder Learning Dialogues. Journal of Business Ethics. 41(1/2).

Davis, Scott; Dunn, Michael. (2002). Building the Brand-Driven Business: Operationalize your brand to drive profitable growth.

Destination 360. (2009). Shopping in Cuba. Destination 360. Retrieved: August 3, 2009. www.destination360.com.

Dickie, Mure; Nuttal, Chris. (2006). EBay Tries to Fix its Strategy in China. Financial Times. Retrieved ProQuest: November 21, 2008. ProQuest document ID: 1183697321.

Doebele, Justin. (2005). Standing Up to EBay. Forbes. Retrieved November 21, 2008. http://www.forbes.com/forbes/2005/0418/050.html.

Doing Business. (2008). Doing Business 2008. Retrieved: August 4, 2009. www.doingbusiness.com.

Duarte de Abreu Filhou, Gilberto; Calicchio, Nicola; Lunardini, Fernando (2003). Brand building in emerging markets. The McKinsey Quarterly. pp. 7-8.

Dumpala, Preethi. (2009). Twitter Business Tool CoTweet Raises $1.1 Million. The Business Insider. July 2, 2009. Retrieved: August 24, 2009. www.businessinsider.com.

Dyer, Davis; Dalzell, Frederick; Olegario, Rowena. (2004). Rising Tide: Lessons from 165 Years of Brand Building at Procter and Gamble. Harvard Business School Press. Retrieved: June 8, 2009. www.wikipedia.org.

Economist. (2007). Tesco Comes to America. The Economist. Retrieved November 27, 2008. http://www.economist.com/displaystory.cfm?story_id=9358986.

Economist. (2008). Business. Economist.com. Retrieved: August 3, 2009. www.economist.com.

Economy Watch. (2009). Free Market Economy. Economy Watch. Retrieved: July 23, 2009. www.economywatch.com.

Emery, David. (1998). Trademark of the Beast. Retrieved: June 8, 2009. www.wikipedia.org.

Emissions Study. (2008). CDP, Supply Chains, Emissions, and Climate Change. Triple Pundit. May 1, 2008. Retrieved: June 8, 2009. www.wikipedia.org.

Encyclopedia of Educational Technology. (2009). Behaviorism: Reinforcement and Punishment. Encyclopedia of Educational Technology. Retrieved: July 26, 2009. www.coe.sdsu.edu.

Encyclopedia of the Nations. (2009). Cuba- Domestic Trade. Encyclopedia of the Nations. Retrieved: July 23, 2009. www.nationsencyclopedia.com.

Erondu, Emmanuel; Sharland, Alex; Okpara, John. (2004). Corporate Ethics in Nigeria. Journal of Business Ethics. 51(4).

Eurofood. (2002). Convenience Boost for Tesco- Tesco PLC Acquires One Stop, Day and Nite Convenience Stores from T. and S. Stores PLC. Eurofood. Retrieved: June 8, 2009. www.wikipedia.org.

Fairclough, Gordon; Fowler, Geoffrey. (2007). Pigs Get the Ax in China. Wall Street Journal. pp. 1-3. Retrieved ProQuest: May 16, 2008. ProQuest document ID: 1201807851.

Ferret.com. (2008). Nestle: Global brand with Asian Signature. Retrieved: May 16, 2008. http://www.ferret.com.au.

Financial Wire Feed. (2006). EBay, TOM Online Go After Growing Chinese Market. Financial Wire. Retrieved ProQuest: November 21, 2008. ProQuest document ID: 1183148721.

FITA. (2009). Introduction to Cuba. FITA. Retrieved: July 23, 2009. www.fita.org.

Food and Drink Europe. (2005). Tesco Builds Korean Business. Food and Drink Europe. www.foodanddrinkeurope.com. Retrieved: June 8, 2009. www.wikipedia.org.

Food Business Review. (2008). Retrieved: June 8, 2009. www.wikipedia.org.

Foodindustry.com. (2006). Tesco Falls Foul of Slovak Government. Foodindustry.com. Retrieved: June 8, 2009. www.wikipedia.org.

Fortune: America's Most Admired Companies 2007. (2008). Retrieved: June 8, 2009. www.wikipedia.org.

Fox, Suzanne. (2008). China's Changing Culture and Etiquette. The China Business Review. 35(4). pg. 48. Retrieved ProQuest: November 26, 2008. ProQuest document ID: 1517455181.

Frank, Marc. (2009). Cuba Struggling to Pay Off Debts. Havana Journal. June 10, 2009. Retrieved: July 23, 2009. www.havanajournal.com.

Franks, Jeff. (2009). Castro Hints at more Belt-tightening for Cuba. Reuters. July 26, 2009. Retrieved: July 27, 2009. www.reuters.com.

Frey, George. (2008). The Sweet Taste of Success. Barron's. 88(18). pp. 18-20. Retrieved ProQuest: May 16, 2008. ProQuest document ID: 1475384951.

Frontline. (2004). The Rise of Wal-Mart. Frontline: Is Wal-Mart Good for America? www.pbs.org. Retrieved: June 8, 2009. www.wikipedia.org.

Gao, Tao. (2004). The Contingency Framework of Foreign Entry Mode Decisions. Multinational Business Review. 12(1).

Gaw, Bill. (2009). Customer Connectivity- The Key to Optimizing Customer Satisfaction. Successful Office. Retrieved: June 8, 2009. www.successfuloffice.com.

Gershon, Howard; Buerstatte. (2003). The E in Marketing: Ethics in the Age of Misbehavior. Journal of Healthcare Management. 48(5).

Giridharadas, A.; Rai, S. (2006). Wal-Mart to Open Hundreds of Stores in India. The New York Times. November 27, 2006. Retrieved: June 8, 2009. www.wikipedia.org.

Gladwell, Malcolm. (2005). Blink. The Power of Thinking Without Thinking. Little, Brown, and Company.

Global Powers of Retailing 2009. Deloitte and Touche. pp. 26-35.

Goett, Pamela. (1999). Michael E. Porter: A Man with a Competitive Advantage. The Journal of Business Strategy. pg. 2.

Goliath. (2003). Tesco to Buy Controlling Stake in Kipa. Goliath World News. www.goliath.ecnext.com. Retrieved: June 8, 2009. www.wikipedia.org.

Google Talking Tales. (2008). Retrieved: December 18, 2008. http://www.google.com/imgres?imgurl=http://talkingtails.files.wordpress.com/2007/07/800px

maslows_hierarchy_of_needssvg.png%3Fw%3D399%26h%3D266&imgrefurl=http://talking
tails.wordpress.com/2007/07/23/maslow-greek-philosophy-indian-
mysticism/&h=524&w=800&sz=147&tbnid=ONkXJi1FwALDuM::&tbnh=94&tbnw=143&prev
=/images%3Fq%3Dmaslow%2527s%2Bhierarchy%2Bof%2Bneeds%2Bpicture&hl=en&usg
=__aUT71EO4f0lY_Omcy4jHnz-
2R84=&sa=X&oi=image_result&resnum=1&ct=image&cd=1

Granitz, Neil. (2003). Individual, Social, and Organizational Sources of Sharing. Journal of
Business Ethics. 42(2).

Grogg, Patricia. (2009). Economy- Cuba: Does the Ration Book Still Make Sense? IPS
News. May 20, 2009. Retrieved: July 23, 2009. www.ipsnews.net.

Guay, Terrence; Doh, Jonathan; Sinclair, Graham. (2004). Non-Governmental
Organizations, Shareholder Activism, and Socially Responsible Investments. Journal of
Business Ethics. 52(1).

Guild, Todd. (2003). Branding's new math. The McKinsey Quarterly 2003 (4). pg. 4.

Haar, Jerry. (2009). Cuba's Business Environment: A Risky Proposition. Revista Inter-
Forum. Retrieved: July 23, 2009. www.revistainterforum.com.

Habiger, Sheldon. (2005). Opening the Door to China. Functional Food & Nutraceuticals.
Retrieved ProQuest: November 26, 2008. ProQuest document ID: 940895961.

Hampton, Jack. (2009). Five Star Global Management Class PowerPoint and Discussion.
July 20-22, 2009. St. John's University.

Harnick, Chris. (2009). New iPhone app launches to connect marketers. Mobile Marketer.
August 17, 2009. Retrieved: August 24, 2009. www.mobilemarketer.com.

Helms, Marilyn. (2003. The Challenge of Entrepreneurship in a Developed Economy: The
Problematic Case of Japan. Journal of Developmental Entrepreneurship. 8(3).

Hein, Kenneth. (2007). Teen Talk is Like, Totally Branded. Brandweek. 48(29). pg. 4.

Heynike, Petrae. (2008). 141st Annual general Meeting of Nestle S.A.- Speech addressed
by   Petrae   Heynike.   Retrieved: May   16,   2008.
http://www.nestle.com/MediaCenter/SpeechesAndStatements.

Hirsch, Jerry. (2008). Tough Sell for Fresh & Easy. Los Angeles Times. Retrieved
November 27, 2008. http://articles.latimes.com/2008/apr/01/business/fi-fresh1.

Hoggan, Karen. (1998). Tesco Tycoon: Interview with Tesco's Fortunes Chairman Ian
MacLaurin. Marketing. Retrieved: June 8, 2009. www.wikipedia.org.

Hou, Jianwei. (2007). Price Determinants in Online Auctions: A Comparative Study of EBay
China and US. Journal of Electronic Commerce Research. Retrieved ProQuest: November
21, 2008. ProQuest document ID: 1330798481.

Houston Business Journal. (2009). Report: New Twitter Tool to Monitor Business Strategy.
Houston Business Journal. August 24, 2009. Retrieved: August 24, 2009.
www.bizjournals.com.

Hughes, Jeff. (2009). App Marketing 101: Introduction to iPhone App Marketing. 148Apps.biz. May 18, 2009. Retrieved: August 24, 2009. www.148apps.biz.

Hugues, Joublin. (2009). L'aventure du premier hyper. L'Expansion. Retrieved: June 8, 2009. www.wikipedia.org.

Hummels, Harry; Timmer, Diederik. (2004). Investors in Need of Social, Ethical, and Environmental Information. Journal of Business Ethics. 52(1).

InBev Personal Interview (2008). Doug Corbett, President InBev International. July, 2008.

Indian Coke. (2003). Indian Coke, Pepsi Laced with Pesticides, Says NGO. Inter Press Service. Retrieved: June 8, 2009. www.wikipedia.org.

Iyer, Gopalkrishnan. (1999). Business, Consumers and Sustainable Living in an Interconnected World. Journal of Business Ethics. 20(4).

Jurkiewicz, Carole; Giacalone, Robert. (2004). A Values Framework for Measuring the Impact of Workplace Spirituality on Organizational Performance. Journal of Business Ethics. 49(2).

Just-food. (2008). US: Wal-Mart Prepares First Marketside Openings. Just-food.com. Retrieved November 27, 2008. http://www.just-food.com/article.aspx?id=103867.

Karande, Kiran; Rao, CP; Singhapakdi. (2002). Moral Philosophies of Marketing Managers. European Journal of Marketing. 36(7/8).

Kaye, Jennifer. (2004). Coca-Cola India. Tuck School of Business at Dartmouth. Retrieved: June 8, 2009. www.wikipedia.org.

Kim, Chong; McInerney, Margie; Sikula, Andrew. (2004). A Model of Reasoned Responses. Journal of Business Ethics. 51(4).

Kimes, Mina. (2009). Fluor's Corporate Crime Fighter. Fortune. www.fortune.ca. Retrieved: February 9, 2009.

Knight, Gary. (2000). Entrepreneurship and Marketing Strategy: The SME Under Globalization. Journal of International Marketing. 8(2).

Knight, Kristina. (2009). Report: Mobile to Become Personal Advertising. Biz Report. August 21, 2009. Retrieved: August 24, 2009. www.bizreport.com.

Kollbrunner, Marcus. (2009). 50 Years Since the Revolution. Socialistworld.net: website of the committee for a workers' international. January 21, 2009. Retrieved: July 23, 2009. www.socialistworld.net.

Kraft Foods. (2002). Kraft Foods Company History. Funding Universe. Retrieved: June 8, 2009. www.wikipedia.org.

Kraft Personal Interview. (2008). Dino Bianco, President Kraft Canada. May, 2008.

Kraft Personal Interview. (2008). Cathy Webster. Vice President Human Resources, Kraft Canada. August 12, 2008.

Kraft Personal Interview. (2009). Dino Bianco, President Kraft Canada. August, 2009.

Kujala, Johanna. (2003). Understanding Managers' Moral Decision-Making. International Journal of Value-Based Management. 16(1).

Kuratko, Donald; Ireland, Duane; Hornsby, Jeffrey. (2001). Improving Firm Performance Through Entrepreneurial Actions: Acordia's Corporate Entrepreneurship Strategy. The Academy Of Management Executive. 15(4).

Labott, Elise. (2009). In Havana, United States turns off sign critical of Cuban government. CNN.com. July 27, 2009. Retrieved: July 28, 2009. www.cnn.com.
Landers, Dezmon. (2008). iPhone Apps as Marketing Tools. StartupHustle. July 16, 2008. Retrieved: August 24, 2009. www.startuphustle.com.

Lazar, Kay. (2004). Harvard Study Links Coca-Cola to Diabetes, Weight Gain. Boston Herald. www.indiaresource.org. Retrieved: January 20, 2009.

Lee, Jung-Wan; Tai, Simon. (2006). Young Consumers' Perceptions of Multinational Firms and their Acculturation Channels Towards Western Products in Transition Economies. International Journal of Emerging Markets. 1(3). pp. 212-220. Retrieved ProQuest: May 16, 2008. ProQuest document ID: 1139365911.

Leggatt, Helen. (2008). Twitter as a Marketing Tool? Biz Report. September 15, 2008. Retrieved: August, 24, 2009. www.bizreport.com.

Leggatt, Helen. (2009). E-mail Sharing via Socnets Being Overlooked by Marketers. Biz Report. August 20, 2009. Retrieved: August 24, 2009. www.bizreport.com.

LeVeness, Frank; Primeaux, Patrick. (2004). Vicarious Ethics: Politics, Business, and Sustainable Development. Journal of Business Ethics. 51(2).

Lewis, Helen. (2007). Global Market Review of New Product Development Strategies. Just-Food. pp. 57-81. Retrieved ProQuest: May 16, 2008. ProQuest document ID: 1400542841.

Li, Mingsheng. (2008). When in China.... Communication World. pg. 34. 25(6). Retrieved ProQuest: November 26, 2008. ProQuest document ID: 1595306591.

Library of Congress. (1996). Russia. Library of Congress Country Studies. July 31, 1996. Retrieved: August 31, 2009. www.lcweb2.loc.gov.

Liverpool Daily Post. (2006). Tesco in Poland Bid. Liverpool Daily Post. www.liverpooldailypost.co.uk. Retrieved: June 8, 2009. www.wikipedia.org.

Lindgreen, Adam. (2004). Corruption and Unethical Behavior. Journal of Business Ethics. 51(1).

Longo, Don. (2007). Gasoline a Logical Extension of Wal-Mart's Reach. Convenience Store News. November 1, 2007. Retrieved: June 8, 2009. www.wikipedia.org.

Lovell, Alan. (2002). Ethics as a Dependent Variable in Individual and Organizational Decision Making. Journal of Business Ethics. 37(2).

Lu, Jiangyong; Tao, Zhigang. (2007). EBay's Strategy in China: Alliance or Acquisition. Asia Case Research Centre. Class case-study.

Lumpkin, GT; Dess, Gregory. (1996). Clarifying the Entrepreneurial Orientation Construct and Linking it to Performance. Academy of Management Review. 21(1).

Maaruthi. (2007). The Cultural Web. Maaruthi Wordpress. Retrieved: July 7, 2008. www.maaruthi.wordpress.com.

Mahmud, Shahnaz. (2008, March). The Inside Job. Adweek, 49(11), 14-15. Retrieved April 24, 2008, from ABI/INFORM Global database. (Document ID: 1462551571).

Martin, Kirsten; Freeman, Edward. (2003). Some Problems with Employee Monitoring. Journal of Business Ethics. 43(4).

McAleer, Sean. (2003). Friedman's Stockholder Theory of Corporate Moral Responsibility. Teaching Business Ethics. 7(4).

McKinley, James. (2007). For United States Exporters in Cuba, Business Trumps Politics. The New York Times. November 12, 2007. Retrieved: July 23, 2009. www.nytimes.com.

McKinsey Quarterly. (2007). How half the world shops: Apparel in Brazil, China, and India. McKinsey Quarterly. pp. 1-13. www.mckinseyquarterly.com.

McPherson, Marianne. (2005). www.ourbodiesourselves.org. Retrieved: June 8, 2009. www.wikipedia.org.

Meacham, Jon; Thomas, Evan. (2009). Newsweek Article. Newsweek. February 16, 2009. Retrieved: August 3, 2009. www.newsweek.com.

Meade, Birgit; Rosen, Stacy. (1997). The Influence of Income on Global Food Spending. Economic Research Service/ USDA. Retrieved: May 16, 2008. http://www.ers.usda.gov.

Mendhro, Umaimah; Sinha, Abhinav. (2009). Three Keys to Staying Ethical in the Age of Madoff. Forbes. www.forbes.com. Retrieved: February 9, 2009.

Mittelstaedt, Fred. (2004). Research and Ethical Issues Related to Retirement Plans. Journal of Business Ethics. 52(2).

Montgomery, Alan. (2001). Applying Quantitative Marketing Techniques to the Internet. Interfaces. 31(2). Retrieved: June 8, 2009. www.wikipedia.org.

Morningnewsbeat.com. (2009. Retrieved: June 9, 2009. www.morningnewsbeat.com.

Morrow, JL. (2002). Someone Old or Someone New?: The Effects of CEO Change on Corporate Entrepreneurship. New England Journal of Entrepreneurship. 5(2).

MSNBC. (2005). Is Wal-Mart Going Green? MSNBC. October 25, 2005. www.msnbc.com. Retrieved: June 8, 2009. www.wikipedia.org.

MSNBC. (2006). Wal-Mart Turns Attention to Upscale Shoppers. MSNBC. March 23, 2006. Retrieved: June 8, 2009. www.wikipedia.org.

Mullen, Megan Gwynne. (2003). A Scheduling and Programming Innovator. The Rise of Cable Programming in the United States: Revolution or Evolution? www.books.google.com. Retrieved: June 8, 2009. www.wikipedia.org.

Murphy, James. (2007). Struggling EBay Inks TOM Deal. Media. Retrieved ProQuest: November 21, 2008. ProQuest document ID: 1212323951.

Nadu, Tamil. (2004). Incidence of Diabetes in India Underestimated. The Hindu. www.hindu.com. Retrieved: January 20, 2009.

Nestle SA website. (2008). Retrieved: December 22, 2008. http://www.nestle.com/Brands/Brands.html

Nestle SA website. (2008). Financial Statements 2008. www.nestle.com. Retrieved: June 8, 2009. www.wikipedia.com.

Nestle Investor Relations. (2008). Nestle Management Report 2007.

Nestle Personal Interview. (2008). Bob Leonidas, President Nestle Canada. May 12, 2008.

Nestle Personal Interview. (2008). Bob Leonidas, President Nestle Canada. August 5, 2008.

Nestle Personal Interview. (2009). Bob Leonidas, President Nestle Canada. August 2, 2009.

Nestle Press Release. (2002). Nestle and Ethiopia: A Statement by Nestle CEO Peter Brabeck. Retrieved: June 8, 2009. www.wikipedia.org.

Nestle Public Affairs. (2008). The Nestle Creating Shared Value Report.

Nestle UK Partners Blend. (2007). About Our Brands. Nestle.co.uk. Retrieved: June 8, 2009. www.wikipedia.org.

New York Times. (1996). Unilever Agrees to Buy Helene Curtis. New York Times. Retrieved: June 8, 2009. www.wikipedia.org.

Nielsen. (2009). Walmart Mid-Year Review. Nielsen. Special Report July, 2009.

Nielsen. (2019). Total CPG Report. July, 2019. https://www.nielsen.com/us/en/insights/report/2019/total-consumer-report-2019/?utm_source=sfmc&utm_medium=email&utm_campaign=newswire&utm_content=8-21-19

NIVEA: Widespread allure. (2007, September). Marketing Week,26. Retrieved May 16, 2008, from ABI/INFORM Global database. (Document ID: 1335546331).

NPR Article. (2008). In Cairo Slum, the Poor Spark Environmental Change. NPR. April 27, 2008. Retrieved: June 8, 2009. www.wikipedia.org.

Oates, John. (2007). Amazon Ups Spending In China. Financial News. Retrieved November 21, 2008. http://www.theregister.co.uk/2007/06/05/amazon_china/print.html.

On Facebook, Ad Sales and the Games People Play. (2008, March). MIN's B 2 B, 11(8), pg 1. Retrieved April 24, 2008, from ABI/INFORM Trade & Industry database. (Document ID: 1438450941).

Ong, Rebecca. (2008). Doing Business 2008: Making a Difference. International Finance Corporation: Creating Opportunity. Retrieved: August 3, 2009. www.ifc.org.

Orr, Deborah. (2006). Slave Chocolate? Retrieved: June 8, 2009. www.wikipedia.org. Oxford English Dictionary. (2008). http://www.en.wikipedia.org/wiki/Brand. Retrieved April 26, 2008.

Peng, Yusheng. (2004). Kinship networks and Entrepreneurs in China's Transitional Economy. The American Journal of Sociology. 109(5).

Pepsico Article. Retrieved: June 8, 2009. www.wikipedia.org.

PepsiCo Personal Interview. (2008). Interview with Marc Guay, President of Pepsico Canada. August 11, 2008.

Pepsico Personal Interview. (2009). Interview with Donna Hrinak, Senior Director, Latin America Government Affairs, Pepsico. September 3, 2009.

Pepsico Press Release. (2009). Pepsico Agrees to Acquire Amacoco, Brazil's Largest Water Company. Retrieved: August 12, 2009. www.finance.yahoo.com.

PepsiCo Program Sessions. (2005). Pepsico International Program Sessions. October 12-13, 2005.

Pepsico Values Guide. (2008).
Pet Food and Pet Care Products in Venezuela. (2008). Retrieved: June 8, 2009. www.wikipedia.org.
Planet Retail. (2009). Daily News by Planet Retail. Retrieved: June 23, 2009. www.planetretail.net.

Planet Retail. (2009). Daily News by Planet Retail. Retrieved: July 1, 2009. www.planetretail.net.

Planet Retail. (2009). Daily News by Planet Retail. Retrieved: August 19, 2009. www.planetretail.net.

Planet Retail. (2009). Daily News by Planet Retail. Retrieved: August 24, 2009. www.planetretail.net.

Planet Retail. (2009). Global Channel Strategies. Planet Retail Global Trends Report. Planet Retail Limited. London, UK.

Premeaux, Shane. (2004). The Current Link Between Management Behavior and Ethical Philosophy. Journal of Business Ethics. 51(3).

Price Chopper Branding PowerPoint. (2009).

Procter and Gamble Annual Report. (2008). Letter from A.G. Lafley. Retrieved: June 8, 2009. www.wikipedia.org.

Procter and Gamble Document. (2005). Finding Alternatives for Product Safety Testing. Procter and Gamble Publication. www.wikipedia.org.

Procter and Gamble Personal Interview. (2008). Tim Penner, President Procter and Gamble Canada.

Procter and Gamble's Purpose, Values, and Principles. (2008).

Qin, Juying. (2007). TOM Online to Shop for Success in China. Wall Street Journal. Retrieved ProQuest: November 21, 2008. ProQuest document ID: 1204445671.

Quenqua, Douglas. (2008). Study: Majority Use Social Media to "Vent" About Customer Care. The ClickZ Network. pg. 1.

Radwan, Sam. (2008). Exporting Growth Strategies. Best's Review. 108(9). Retrieved ProQuest: November 26, 2008. ProQuest document ID: 1412236901.

Renton, Jennifer; Binedell, Nick. (2002). World Marketing Guru Kevin Lane Keller Presents Lessons on Strategic Brand Management. Gale Group PR Newswire. pp. 1-2.

Reuters. (2008). Tesco to Buy Thirty-Six South Korean Stores. Reuters. www.uk.reuters.com. Retrieved: June 8, 2009. www.wikipedia.org.

Roberts, Dexter; Rocks, David. (2005). Let a Thousand Brands Bloom. Business Week. Issue 3955. pp. 58-62. Retrieved ProQuest: May 16, 2008. ProQuest document ID: 910537261.

Romar, Edward. (2004). Managerial Harmony: The Confucian Ethics of Peter F. Drucker. Journal of Business Ethics. 51(2).

Rowley, Jennifer. (2004). Online Branding. Online Information Review. 28(2). pg. 131.

Ruettgers, Mike. (2003). Responsibility Lies in Leadership. Vital Speeches of the Day. 70(5).

Sacramento Business Journal. (2008). Analyst: Tesco's Fresh & Easy Stores in Trouble. Sacramento Business Journal. Retrieved November 27, 2008. http://www.bizjournals.com/sacramento/stories/2008/03/10/daily57.html?ana=from_rss.

Sama, Linda; Shoaf, Victoria. (2002). Ethics on the Web. Journal of Business Ethics. 36(1/2).

Schindehutte, Minet; Morris, Michael; Kuratko, Donald. (2000). Triggering Events, Corporate Entrepreneurship and the Marketing Function. Journal of Marketing Theory and Practice. 8(2).

Schultz, Don. (2002, Sept/ Oct). Who Owns the Brand? Marketing Management, (11)5, pg 9.

Schwepker, Charles. (2003). An Exploratory Investigation of the Relationship Between Ethical Conflict and Salesperson Performance. The Journal of Business and Industrial Marketing. 18(4/5).

Sell, Hannah. (2009). Socialism in the Twenty-First Century. Socialist Party- World Analysis. Retrieved: August 2, 2009. www.socialistparty.com.

Shackelford, David. (2009). Facebook Groups: E-Mail Marketing, Evolved. Shack Attack: Social Media. April 24, 2009. Retrieved: August 21, 2009. www.dshack.net.

Shaw, Deirdre; Shiu, Edward. (2003). Ethics in Consumer Choice. European Journal of Marketing. 37(10).

ShopSavvy. (2009). The final frontier: Groceries! ShopSavvy. April 8, 2009. Retrieved: August 21, 2009. www.biggu.com.

Simms, Jane. (2007, December). Brands we love... ...and brands we hate. Marketing, 51-52. Retrieved April 24, 2008, from ABI/INFORM Global database. (Document ID: 1415779871).

Simons, Ross. (2008). The Four Levers of Control. Retrieved July 5, 2008. http://maaruthi.wordpress.com/2007/06/10/the-cultural-web/.

Singh, Navjit. (2008). Corporate Strategy: Best Practice- Perfect Landing. Foreign Direct Investment. Retrieved ProQuest: November 21, 2008. ProQuest document ID: 1574165971.

SinoCast China (2007). EBay CEO Has Something to Say About Free Policy. SinoCast China Business Daily News. Retrieved ProQuest: November 21, 2008. ProQuest document ID: 1301704891.

SinoCast China (2007). EBay Confident in JV with TOM Online. SinoCast China Business Daily News. Retrieved ProQuest: November 21, 2008. ProQuest document ID: 1232016671.

SinoCast China. (2007). Former eBay China President Joins Matrix Partners. SinoCast China Business Daily News. Retrieved ProQuest: November 21, 2008. ProQuest document ID: 1292628341.

SinoCast China (2007). Google China to Have 500-Plus Employees at Year-End. SinoCast China Business Daily News. Retrieved ProQuest: November 21, 2008. ProQuest document ID: 1290392381.

Snell, Robin; Herndon, Neil. (2004). Hong Kong's Code of Ethics Initiative. Journal of Business Ethics. 51(1).

Snopes. (2007). Coca-Cola and Israel. www.snopes.com. Retrieved: June 8, 2009. www.wikipedia.org.

Sparkes, Russell; Cowton, Christopher. (2004). The Maturing of Socially Responsible Investment. Journal of Business Ethics. 52(1).
Spickett-Jones, Graham; Kitchen, Philip; Reast, Jon. (2003). Social Facts and Ethical Hardware. Journal of Communication Management. 8(1).

Sporting Clube de Portugal. (2009). Retrieved: June 8, 2009. www.wikipedia.org.

Srnka, Katharina. (2004). Culture's Role in Marketers' Ethical Decision Making. Academy of Marketing Science Review.

Stovall, Scott; Neill, John; Perkins, David. (2004). Corporate Governance, Internal Decision Making, and the Invisible Hand. Journal of Business Ethics. 51(2).

Supermarket News. (2009). Wal-Mart Debuts Club Store for Hispanics. Supermarket News. Retrieved: August 10, 2009. www.supermarketnews.com.

Tamayo, Juan. (2009). Less Phones Per Capita in Cuba Now Than in 1958. Havana Journal. July 23, 2009. Retrieved: July 23, 2009. www.havanajournal.com.

Taylor, Charles. (2008). Lifestyle Matters Everywhere- Marketers Need to Stop Targeting Consumers by Country and Instead Target Based on Habits, Likes, Dislikes. AdAge.com. pp. 1-5. Retrieved: May 20, 2008. http://adage.com/cmostrategy.

Tesco (2006). Tesco Announces Non-Food Store Trials. Tesco. www.tescocorporate.com. Retrieved: June 8, 2009. www.wikipedia.org.

Tesco. (2008). Tesco Careers- Human Resources. Tesco. www.tesco-graduates.com. Retrieved: June 8, 2009. www.wikipedia.org.

Tesco. (2006). Tesco DVD Rental. Tesco. www.tescodvdrental.com. Retrieved: June 8, 2009. www.wikipedia.org.

Tesco. (2006). Tesco Our History. Tesco PLC. www.tescocorporate.com. Retrieved: June 8, 2009. www.wikipedia.org.

Tesco Hungary. (2008). Tesco Services. Tesco Hungary. www.tesco.hu. Retrieved: June 8, 2009. www.wikipedia.org.

Tesco Lotus. (2008). Key Facts About Tesco Lotus. Tesco Lotus. www.tescolotus.net. Retrieved: June 8, 2009. www.wikipedia.org.

Tesco Personal Interview. August 3, 2009. Daniel Gilsenan, Director of Business Development, Tesco.

Tesco Poland. (2008). About Tesco Poland. Tesco Poland. www.tesco.pl. Retrieved; June 8, 2009. www.wikipedia.org.

That Which People Eat. (2009).

The Economist. (2007). No Ketchup, Please. The Economist. www.economist.com. Retrieved: June 8, 2009. www.wikipedia.org.

The Guardian. (2007). PDF of The 2006 Giving List. The Guardian. www.image.guardian.co.uk. Retrieved: June 6, 2009. www.wikipedia.org.

The Guardian. (2009). Tesco Unveils Record Profits of 3 Billion Pounds. The Guardian. April, 2009. Retrieved: June 8, 2009. www.wikipedia.org.

The Times. (2008). Monday Manifesto: Unilever Chairman Michael Treschow. The Times. May 26, 2008.

The Times. (2008). Tesco Express Rolls Into China. The Times. www.business.timesonline.co.uk. Retrieved: June 8, 2009. www.wikipedia.org.

Third World Traveler. (1997). A Historical Look at the Pepsico/ Burma Boycott. Third World Traveler. www.thirdworldtraveler.com. Retrieved: June 8, 2009. www.wikipedia.org.

Thomasson, Emma. (2009). Nestlé's Nespresso Sees Double Digit Sales Growth. Reuters.com. Retrieved: June 10, 2009.

Thornberry, Neal. (2003). Corporate Entrepreneurship: Teaching Managers to be Entrepreneurs. The Journal of Management Development. 22(4).

Thuermer, Karen E. (2007, August). Cover Story: Cobra Beer - From small beer. Foreign Direct Investment,1. Retrieved May 16, 2008, from ABI/INFORM Global database. (Document ID: 1320281921).

Toma, Glenda. Thred Up Unveils a New Platform and $175 Million in Funding as Resale Trend Accelerates. Forbes. August 21, 2019. https://www.forbes.com/sites/glendatoma/2019/08/21/thredup-resale-175-million-funding/#21d05d68beb7

Tong, Tony; Reuer, Jeffrey; Peng, Mike. (2008). International Joint Ventures and the Value of Growth Options. Academy of Management Journal. 51(5). Retrieved ProQuest: November 21, 2008. ProQuest document ID: 1594616781.

Travel Document Systems. (2009). Cuba North America. Travel Document Systems. Retrieved: July 23, 2009. www.traveldocs.com.

Trunick, Perry. (2006). Wal-Mart Reinvents Itself in China. Newsweek. October 30, 2006. Retrieved: June 8, 2009. www.wikipedia.org.

Tucker, Robert. (2002). Adding Value Profitability. The American Salesman.

TweetPR. (2009). Debunking the Social Media Barriers. TweetPR. Retrieved: August 21, 2009. www.tweetpr.com.

Unilever. (2008). Unilever has announced its intention to have all of its palm oil certified sustainable by 2015. www.unilever.com. Retrieved: June 8, 2009. www.wikipedia.org.

Unilever Annual Report. (2008). Annual Report. Retrieved: June 8, 2009. www.wikipedia.org.
Unilever Disrobed. (2008). Unilever Disrobed: Interview with Dove/ Axe Mashup Artist. Retrieved: June 8, 2009. www.wikipedia.org.

Unilever Heartbrand. (2006). Unilever Heartbrand. Retrieved: June 8, 2009. www.wikipedia.org.

Unilever Personal Interview. (2008). Jeffrey Allgrove, Senior Vice President Unilever Brand Integration. July 29, 2008.

Unilever Personal Interview. (2009). David Blanchard, President Unilever Canada. August 10, 2009.

Unilever Powerpoint. (2009). Document presented to Price Chopper May, 2009.

United States Bureau of Western Hemisphere Affairs. (2008). Background Note: Cuba. Bureau of Western Hemisphere Affairs: United States Department of State. Retrieved: July 23, 2009. www.state.gov.

University of Massachusetts Amherst study. (2006). Political Economy Research Institute Toxic 100. Retrieved: June 8, 2009. www.wikipedia.org.

USA Today. (2005). Viral Advertising Spreads Through Marketing Plans. USA Today. www.usatoday.com. Retrieved: June 8, 2009. www.wikipedia.org.

USDA. (2008). http://www.ers.usda.gov/publications/agoutlook/jul1997/ao242e.pdf. pg. 14. Retrieved May 16, 2008.

Valentine, Sean; Godkin, Lynn; Lucero, Margaret. (2002). Ethical Context, Organizational Commitment, and Person-Organization Fit. Journal of Business Ethics. 41(4).

Velasquez, Manuel. (2001). Business Ethics: Concepts and Cases (5th Edition). Prentice Hall.

Walden, Jamie. (2008). Confucius Institute Helps Arkansas Companies Go Global. Arkansas Business. 25(41). pg. 16. Retrieved ProQuest: November 26, 2008. ProQuest document ID: 1590508371.

Wallis, William; Mahtani, Dino. (2007). Ivory Coast: Cocoa Exports Fund Ivory Coast Conflict. Retrieved: June 8, 2009. www.wikipedia.org.

Wal-Mart Annual Report. (2006). Wal-Mart 2006 Annual Report. Wal-Mart. Retrieved: June 8, 2009. www.wikipedia.org.

Wal-Mart Facts. (2006). The Wal-Mart Timeline. www.walmartfacts.com. Retrieved: June 8, 2009. www.wikipedia.org.

Wal-Mart SEC. (2006). Wal-Mart SEC Form 10-K. United States Securities and Exchange Commission. January 31, 2006. Retrieved: June 8, 2009. www.wikipedia.org.

Wal-Mart Watch. (2008). Shareholder Information. www.walmartwatch.com. Retrieved: February 11, 2009.

Waring, Peter; Lewer, John. (2004). The Impact of Socially Responsible Investment on Human Resource Management. Journal of Business Ethics. 52(1).

Watson, Tony. (2003). Ethical Choice in Managerial Work. Human Relations. 56(2).

Weiss, Gregory. (1999). An Investment in Coca-Cola will be the Real Thing. Investment Quality Trends. www.thebullandbear.com. Retrieved: January 20, 2009.

Wherrity, Constance. (2006). Dial Agrees to Buy Procter and Gamble Deodorant Brands. Pierce Mattie Public Relations New York blog. www.piercemattie.com. Retrieved: June 8, 2009. www.wikipedia.org.

Wikipedia. (2009). Carrefour. Retrieved: June 8, 2009. www.wikipedia.org.

Wikipedia. (2009). Kraft. Retrieved: June 8, 2009. www.wikipedia.org.

Wikipedia. (2009). Nestle. Retrieved: June 8, 2009. www.wikipedia.org.
Wikipedia. (2009). Social Media. Retrieved: June 8, 2009. www.wikipedia.org.

Wikipedia. (2009). Tesco. Retrieved: June 8, 2009. www.wikipedia.org.

Wikipedia. (2009). Wal-Mart. Retrieved: June 8, 2009. www.wikipedia.org.

Wired. (2005). Marketers Feverish Over Viral Ads. www.wired.com. Retrieved: June 8, 2009. www.wikipedia.org.

Wood, Stuart. (2006). Brand Continuity: It's the same, but different. Brand Strategy. pp. 1-3. Retrieved ProQuest: May 16, 2008. ProQuest document ID: 1060502761.

Woodall, Katherine. (2002). Survival- Can Branding Save Your Organization? Communication World. pp. 11-12.

Wordnet.princeton.edu/perl/webwn. Retrieved April 26, 2008.

World Health Organization Fact Sheet. (2008). What is Diabetes? www.who.int. Retrieved: January 20, 2009.

World Socialist Movement. (2009). How the WSM is Different from Other Groups. The World Socialist Movement. Retrieved: August 3, 2009. www.worldsocialism.org.

www.answers.com. Retrieved: January 31, 2009.

www.wordnet.princeton.edu. Retrieved: January 31, 2009.

Yahoo Finance. (2009). Breyers Premieres Latest Webisode Parody Starring Jane Krakowski. Yahoo Finance. Retrieved: June 10, 2009. www.finance.yahoo.com.

Yahoo Finance. (2009). Doritos Breaks New Ground in Fusing Music and Technology by putting Blink-182, big Boi Concerts in the Palms of Fans' Hands. Yahoo Finance. Retrieved: July 6, 2009. www.finance.yahoo.com.

Yahoo Finance. (2009). Key Facts About Russia's Retail Sector. Yahoo Finance- Reuters. September 3, 2009. Retrieved: September 3, 2009. www.reuters.com.

Yahoo Finance. (2009). Russian Equities Could Soar Amid Government Support, Steady Oil. Yahoo Finance. September 3, 2009. Retrieved: September 3, 2009. www.finance.yahoo.com.

Yahoo Finance. (2009). Starbucks Ice Cream Invites Facebook to Treat Friends and Family. Yahoo Finance. Retrieved: July 6, 2009. www.finance.yahoo.com.

Yahoo Finance. (2009). Wal-Mart Stores, Inc. Yahoo Finance. www.finance.yahoo.com. Retrieved: June 8, 2009. www.wikipedia.org.

Yeung, Matthew; Ramasamy, Bala. (2008). Brand value and firm performance nexus: Further empirical evidence. Journal of Brand Management, 15(5), 322-335. Retrieved April 24, 2008, from ABI/INFORM Global database. (Document ID: 1459651371).

Yuthas, Kristi; Dillard, Jesse; Rogers, Rodney. (2004). Beyond Agency and Structure. Journal of Business Ethics. 51(2).

Zook, Matthew; Graham, Mark. (2006). Wal-Mart Nation: Mapping the Reach of a Retail Colossus. Wal-Mart World: The World's Biggest Corporation in the Global Economy. pp. 15-25. Retrieved: June 8, 2009. www.wikipedia.org.

Zyglidopolous, Stelios. (2002). The Social and Environmental Responsibilities of Multinationals. Journal of Business Ethics. 36(1/2).

24/7 Wall Street. (2009). The Future of Twitter- 10 Ways Twitter Will Change American Business. 24/7 Wall St. August 24, 2009. Retrieved: August 24, 2009. www.time.com

Made in United States
Troutdale, OR
01/28/2024